לעילוי נשמת המנוח

ישעיהו בן בנימין ז״ל

The Challenge of God to Man

A Theology of Responsible Freedom

Sidney Breitbart

VANTAGE PRESS
New York

FIRST EDITION

All rights reserved, including the right of
reproduction in whole or in part in any form.

Copyright © 1994 by Sidney Breitbart

Published by Vantage Press, Inc.
516 West 34th Street, New York, New York 10001

Manufactured in the United States of America
ISBN: 0-533-10921-3

Library of Congress Catalog Card No.: 93-95032

0 9 8 7 6 5 4 3 2 1

To the loving memory of my grandson, Michael Joseph Kaplan, a third-year Harvard University student who was killed by a drunken driver

September 29, 1967–March 5, 1988

וַתְּחַסְּרֵהוּ מְּעַט מֵאֱלֹהִים
וְכָבוֹד וְהָדָר תְּעַטְּרֵהוּ:

Yet Thou has made him but little
lower than the angels,
And hast crowned him with glory
and honor.
—Psalm 8:6

There were still so many roads for him to travel and explore . . .

Acknowledgments

I wish to express my sincere appreciation to the following people for the help given to me during the preparation of this book:

Dr. Leivy Smolar, former president of Baltimore Hebrew University, for his encouragement and constructive editing;

Dr. Alan L. Udoff, BHU Louis L. Kaplan Chair in Philosophy, for his critical analysis and suggestions;

Dr. Louis L. Kaplan, president emeritus of Baltimore Hebrew College, for encouraging me to pursue my original ideas;

Jean Bernstein, secretary to the president of Baltimore Hebrew University, for word-processing the entire manuscript from its initial stages through various revisions to completion;

the publishers of *Dor-le-Dor* for permission to use some of my articles published in their magazine;

and my wife, Yvette, for her patience and support during these years of study, research, and writing.

Contents

Foreword by Alan Udoff ... ix
Author's Remarks ... xi

Part A: The Reinterpretation of the Test of Adam and Its Metaphysical Meaning

I. Genesis 1 and 2: Man's Role in the Story of Creation ... 3
II. The Traditional Jewish and Christian Interpretations of the Adam Story ... 10
III. Adam's Resolution of the Test—the New Interpretation of the Test of Adam ... 16
IV. Adam's Choice as the Paradigm of Responsible Freedom ... 28
V. The Akedah: A Test of Abraham as a Partner of God ... 37

Part B: The Application of the Concepts Developed in Part A to Some Religious Aspects

VI. Revelation: Resolving the Conflict in Communication between the Infinite and Finite Orders of Being ... 51
VII. Covenant: Resolving the Disjunction of God and Man ... 56
VIII. Prayer: Addressing the Other in the Partnership of God and Man ... 63
IX. Forgiveness: What Can Be Forgiven and Who Can Forgive ... 67
X. The Question of the Chosen People: The Agent of Choice ... 76
XI. The Jewish and Christian Covenants and the Holocaust: The Role of Covenantal Thinking and the Origin of Auschwitz ... 84

Part C: The Resolution of the Problem of Suffering and Evil Leading to a New Theology as Well as a Theodicy

XII. The Problem of Suffering and Evil in the Theological Tradition — 101

XIII. An Analysis of Job: The Problem of Universality and Particularity in the Book of Job — 118

XIV. The Theological Resolution of the Problem of Evil: The Part Played by Man's Choice and Responsible Freedom — 125

XV. The Problem of Theodicy: Freedom, Responsibility, and Evil — 130

Afterword by Dr. Leivy Smolar — 143

Foreword

We owe to Leo Strauss this observation: "No one can be both a philosopher and a theologian or, for that matter, a third which is beyond the conflict between philosophy and theology, or a synthesis of both. But every one of us can and ought to be either the one or the other; the philosopher open to the challenge of theology or the theologian open to the challenge of philosophy." There is a great deal that would have to be said about this text before it could be considered adequately understood. With respect to the present occasion, this much at any rate is warranted: the excellence of a life may be measured by the extent to which this conflict—the *agon* of Athens and Jerusalem—has been engaged. The book at hand is the result of this engagement.

Over a score of years, as teacher and friend, I have been devoted to the author, and thus the efforts of his writing. Perhaps it will not be out of place to remind the reader what Spinoza says of devotion: it is the form taken by love for those whom we admire. In explanation of this, Spinoza remarks on how wonder (*admiratio*) is linked to the novelty of a thing, and how devotion is altered accordingly as novelty diminishes. It is the mark of the work that is born of the conflict of the openness of philosophy and theology, each vocation open to the evocation of the other, that by virtue of that openness alone, by being reminded of that openness alone, we are, as it were, forever renewed. The reader of this work is reminded, thereby, of that which makes for the highest excellence of a humanly lived life.

As understood by Sidney Breitbart, the conflict of Athens and Jerusalem is concentrated in the question of the human encounter with God conceived as the *partnership* of *ethical relation*. In this sense, his theology belongs to modern—that is to say, post-Kantian Jewish thought—whose most profound expression is articulated in the reflections of Emmanuel Levinas. It is from the Bible, however, that this theology takes its bearings, as time and time again the source of partnership is sought in the reading of Scripture. That reading began for the author as a *turn* to Jewish texts. Under the influence of their teaching, his repeated readings took the course of a *return*. The resonances of this word, its *topos*, should not be lost on the reader—before whom this book stands as the efforts of a man whose years have passed threescore and ten, the sum of which is the excellence of the vocation of their thought.

—Alan Udoff

Author's Remarks

Monotheism is Judaism's notable contribution to Western civilization. It is not God as such, but God in relation to man that is the center of Judaism. Religion begins with the establishment of the correlation between the individual, the community, and God.

Choice is the exercise of freedom. Responsible freedom gives rise to responsible choices. This is the basis of ethics. Living with a sense of responsibility based on responsible freedom expresses God's will.

Two experiences in my life have shaped my thoughts on theology and religion, Christianity and Judaism. These experiences have been the motivation to begin my own search for man's relation to God and to other human beings. The contradictions and inconsistencies within and between the two religions gave impetus to my quest.

My first experience was as a child of about twelve when I witnessed a small pogrom on our street in Lodz, Poland, at the time my father was supposed to return home from work. This made an everlasting impact on my life. I was exposed to anti-Semitism every day and the cry of *"Zydcie"* (a perjorative term for "Jew") still rings in my ears. Why did these things occur? Since the Christians were always the perpetrators, it seemed to me that something was profoundly misconceived in their notion of religion.

The second experience had its roots in my first heart attack, at the age of forty-one. My recuperation gave me the opportunity for a renewed reading of the Torah. Immediately I was struck by apparent inconsistencies and contradictions in the text. The questions of sin, reward, and punishment; the meaning of life; for what purpose were human beings created; does God and can God intervene in human history; and if we Jews were the elect of God, why are we subjected to so many tragedies, especially the Shoah, crowded my thoughts.

This book is the culmination of my efforts to find the answers to these questions.

The Challenge of God to Man

PART A

The Reinterpretation of the Test of Adam and Its Metaphysical Meaning

This section discusses the assignment of the physical world to man by God and the contradictions involved in the Adam test narrative. This leads to a new and novel reinterpretation of the "Test." The result is that a new relationship with God is developed, that of man-God partnership.

Chapter I
Genesis 1 and 2: Man's Role in the Story of Creation

God's meaning for life is the great theme with which Genesis 1 through 3 and parts of 4 deals. Genesis 1 begins with the creation of the world and ends with instruction to man to "have dominion over the earth."[1] While this story is by no means a scientific explanation of creation in a modern sense, it depicts some progression from lower to higher forms of life.

The wording in Genesis 1 is striking in several ways. When creation of natural, inanimate objects and of lower levels of life was taking place, God simply created by saying, "Let there be . . ." When man was to be created, God said, "Let us make man . . . ," a singular difference. God also introduced His *intention* for man prior to the act of creating him (1:26).

Still another concept unique to Genesis 1 followed in the biblical text is "in our image, after our likeness" (1:26). This stamps man in God's likeness and is more than a continuation of physical creation. The text elevates man to a different type of existence from earlier forms. However, it is important to note that Adam *is not* the image of God, but *in* the image of God. Accordingly, "image" relationship has been variously interpreted as reason, free will, creativity, intellect, and imagination. These form the basic framework of man's existence. These attributes share in common the nature of dispensation; each is divinely given as a gift by God to man, which will enable man to fulfill the duties accepted by him, as shown later in this chapter.

The idea of man as being made in the "image" of God was juxtaposed (1:27, 1:28) to the idea that man is responsible for the world. The God-man image, then, is a prerequisite for fulfilling this charge by God. The most noteworthy aspect of Genesis 1 is the charge to man to "master"[2] the world and "rule over it." Adam was not given a choice in the matter (1:28). Since Adam was the only being in existence, the archetype of man, the charge to have dominion over the world applied to all future beings and thus represented a permanent charge. Man, having been given the responsibility for the condition of, as well as dominion over, the world, can then be considered as a partner with God in the physical domain. The terms *master* and *free will* may also imply that God deliberately did not create a perfect world, thus giving man the opportunity to improve on God's creation.

While Genesis 1 qualifies each day of creation by the statement, " . . . and He saw that this was good," no such statement relates to the creation of man. However, in summary, after *all* creation, God says, " . . . that this was *very good*" (emphasis added). This represents a remarkable omission. It may be attributed to the free will of man, which can result in a negative or positive contribution to the state of the world. It is suggested that God's reference to the total creation as very good, a higher level than just good, represents man as a positive ingredient in the totality of creation. If we consider that God, prior to creation, must have made a primal choice of the kind of world He wanted to create, His decision to create man with free will was deliberate, in order to make human life more meaningful. Without free will, man could not *choose* to become God's partner. Man's life would be predetermined, and thus there would be no meaning theologically to his existence.

In the preceding pages, it was argued that Adam I[3] is charged with the responsibility for the physical world. A physical world, however, is not in a state of completion. The spiritual and moral elements have to be introduced into it. This occurs on the seventh day when the dimension of holiness is introduced. This sets the tone for chapter 2 immediately preceding the creation of Adam II.

The creation of Adam II is radically different from the creation of Adam I. Adam II is "formed from the dust of the earth," and God blows into his nostrils the breath of life. God further emphasizes the difference by placing Adam II in the Garden of Eden, which is hardly the place for mastery and dominion, which is the purpose in Genesis 1. In mentioning the "Tree of Knowledge of Good and Evil" immediately in the next sentence, God calls attention to the close connection between the creation of Adam II and the Tree. Indeed, Adam II's function was to consider man's relationship to God in the realm of the moral and spiritual. God's faith in Adam II to achieve this purpose is best illustrated by His asking Adam to name the animals, an act of transcendence and creativity. Adam II's potential is, therefore, made obvious and emphasized.

Adam I was to have dominion over the physical world, while Adam II was to be responsible for the moral and spiritual sphere. The two Adams complement each other and, indeed, may be considered as the two manifestations or phases of man—one concerning itself with his passions, physical requirements, and desires, while the other acts to *control* these by his moral and spiritual views. The conclusion is that the choice made by Adam II was in accordance with God's plan inasmuch as God deliberately introduced factors that were to serve as prerequisites for the proper resolution of the "Test" by Adam II.

Genesis 2 starts with the concept of Sabbath—a day of rest and holiness.

The heaven and the earth were finished, and all their array. On the seventh day God finished the work which He had been doing, and He ceased on the seventh day from all the work which He had done. And God blessed the seventh day and declared it holy, because on it God ceased from all the work of creation which He had done. Such is the story of heaven and earth when they were created.

—Genesis 2:1–4

In contrast to chapter 1, which deals with the physical only, the spiritual and moral dimensions are conspicuous in chapter 2. These act as the counterpoise to limit Adam's freedom of dominion in the physical domain.

Adam II is created from the dust of the earth, thus showing he is a part of nature and that, as such, there is a universal aspect to him. Then God breathes life into him and man becomes a living soul. In this manner, man becomes a spiritual entity, which is of a higher order than the physical.

The difference between the two concepts or views of Adam in Genesis 1 and 2 can also be seen as follows. In Genesis 1, Adam is formed as the *final* act of creation of the world. In Genesis 2, the spiritual Adam is formed before the animal kingdom is created and the reader is prepared for the drama in Genesis 2 and, above all, the Test of Adam.

The story of Eden begins with a description of the significant trees in Eden. After placing Adam II in the Garden of Eden, God challenges Adam II:

And the Lord God commanded the man, saying, "Of every tree of the garden you are free to eat; but as for the tree of knowledge of good and bad, you must not eat of it; for as soon as you eat of it, you shall die."

—Genesis 2:16

The Tree of Knowledge of Good and Evil could be described as representing a tension between desire and conscience, between the earthly and the spiritual parts of man. The biblical text uses these specific terms quite purposefully. The Tree of Knowledge of Good and Evil and death indicate that good, evil, and death are built into the structure of the universe itself prior to man's action.

Adam does not immediately respond to God's command not to eat the fruit of the Tree of Knowledge of Good and Evil. How may we account for this delay? Answering this question requires a review of the whole sequence of the narratives, from Genesis 2 to Genesis 3:1, which indicate that God deliberately introduced factors that, after analysis, would help Adam determine the choices he would make.

The planting of the Tree of Knowledge of Good and Evil (2:9) is immediately followed by rivers arising from the Garden of Eden (2:10):

> The Lord God planted a garden in Eden, in the east, and placed there the man whom He had formed. And from the ground the Lord God caused to grow every tree that was pleasing to the sight and good for food, with the tree of life in the middle of the garden, and the tree of knowledge of good and bad.
>
> A river issues from Eden to water the garden, and it then divides and becomes four branches.
> —Genesis 2:10

Since the river is shown as necessary to water the Garden, it is more so outside the Garden (as evidenced by subdividing the river). This implies that the presence of the rivers will be a factor in Adam's decision; *otherwise, there would be no reason to introduce them prior to the choice.* Since rivers provide water and food, which are necessary ingredients for the survival of man on earth, the mention of a river originating in the Garden, which would extend into the world immediately following the planting of the trees, foretells that the threat of death as a consequence of the choice was not immediate, but that Adam would become a mortal being (an earthling).

God then forms the animals from dust and brings them to Adam to name. In accordance with the ancient belief that naming means conferring meaning and significance, the animals are transcended. God enlists Adam to *finish the act of creation*. The physical world, including man, was created by God without any input by man, but the world of meaning in the process of naming was the task assigned to man.

This act of naming, located between the original order to Adam II and the actual choice by him, *predicts that Adam will make the proper response to the test;* otherwise, man would not be asked to complete the act of creation, nor would the mention of rivers be introduced.

Another factor deserves attention pertaining to God's prediction of Adam's choice. God said; "It is not good for man to be alone. I will make a fitting helper for him" (2:18). This shows that Adam's choice will result in his leaving the garden and assuming an earthly existence; this is the topos where a helper is necessary.

The final factor showing that God indicated that Adam would partake of the fruit of the Tree of Knowledge of Good and Evil and thus become mortal is shown in Genesis 1:28: "Be frutiful and multiply." God's purpose and intent is evident by His endowing Adam and Eve with the potential for reproduction.

This potential for reproduction does not point to immortality; instead, it denotes mortality. There is no need for powers of reproduction if man is to be immortal. It follows that God's design of man implied that Adam would become human; therefore, Adam's choice did not constitute a sin.

The direct charge to Adam in Genesis 1:28 implies change. Change, however, is a vital principle of physical laws that God created. Change causes matter to deteriorate and eventually cease to exist. It follows that in creation God made provision for mortality on a universal scale and, therefore, the threat of death in the Adam test could not be a threat or punishment. Why, then, did

God say, "You shall die," in conjunction with His order not to eat of the fruit of the Tree of Knowledge of Good and Evil? Again, this represented another condition in the test to permit Adam, born with wisdom and intellect, to resolve the problem in accordance with God's purpose. Had God meant immediate death, another creation would have had to take place.

In possession of free will as well as physical desires man can abuse his actions. His physical desires unchecked would very likely take complete control of him. To prevent such a condition, God resorted to the Test of Adam, involving the knowledge of good and evil. It was not a question of whether Adam would do good or evil, but whether he had the ability to discern the difference between them and thus become a moral being. Morality acts as a restraint to man's physical desires.

Notes

1. All references to the Torah are from the Jewish Publication Society translation, 2nd edition (Philadelphia: 1967). Used with permission of the publisher. (All parenthetical references in this book refer to Genesis, unless otherwise stated.)
2. Mastering the world requires the knowledge to understand the processes and laws of nature. Therefore, it is incumbent upon man to study physics, mathematics, and all other physical sciences in order to perform as a partner of God in the physical sphere. In this sense, man must use the resources of nature for the good of mankind, not to destroy them for profit.
3. Adam from Genesis 1 will be referred to as Adam I, while Adam from Genesis 2 will be referred to as Adam II.

Chapter II
The Traditional Jewish and Christian Interpretations of the Adam Story

The interpretation of the Test of Adam in both the Jewish and especially Christian tradition dating back to Augustine is that it represents a "sin," although this word is not mentioned in the Torah. Both the Jewish and Christian views are that although Adam was created as a perfect being, he disobeyed God's command.

The fact that man was created with "free will" casts doubt on his perfection. Thus, after analyzing the test and in the exercise of his free will, he "disobeyed God."

In Maimonidean terms, Adam, through his choice, lost his intellectual perfection (knowing truth and falsity) by acquiring the element of knowing good and evil (practical knowledge), which betrayed his intellectual perfection. Man's attempt since then has been to return to that state of perfection. However, in response to Maimonides, it is questionable whether the element of knowledge of good and evil, having once been acquired, can be separated from man. Furthermore, Maimonides appears to argue that "good and evil," and thus morality, are not necessary for this world.

Judaism claims that Adam's action was a sin that, however, was not inherited by succeeding generations. According to Jewish thought, man is not born with a sinful nature. Universal mortality cannot be the result of Adam's punishment, since God, being just, would not have punished all generations, but only Adam, for what he alone had done. Certainly God would not condemn all human beings for one man's transgression. In my view, mortality was chosen by man himself, autonomously, when Adam chose to have the knowledge of good and evil and thus became the partner of God, responsible for the moral condition of the world and for leading a meaningful life. Furthermore, the claim of sin is not tenable if two statements in the Torah are taken literally. The first says that God made man a little lower than Elohim (a generic term for God or gods) (Psalm 8:6). Then, in Genesis 3:22, God said, "Now that the man has become like one of us, knowing good and evil . . . " The acquisition of knowledge of good and evil elevated man.

How does Christianity deal with Adam's test? The Christian view of man, in accordance with Gospel interpretation of the story, is that man is born with a sinful nature and, therefore, must tend toward sin. Man's propensity to sin is, therefore, not volitional and thus not man's responsibility. In the first few centuries of Christianity there were quite a few dissenters from this viewpoint who emphasized the freedom of man, but Augustine firmly established original sin as the official Catholic Christian view and has greatly influenced Protestant thought.

The Adam test forms the basis of Christianity. According to Gospel teaching, "through one man [Adam], sin entered the world, and through another [Jesus] mankind was redeemed" (Romans 5:18). In the period lasting three hundred years after the death of Jesus, many church fathers professed different opinions. About one hundred years after Jesus' death, the Christians lived in fear of arrest, torture, and execution for refusing allegiance to the emperors and their gods. Justin (circa 110 C.E.) invoked Genesis to argue that humankind owes allegiance only to God, who created humanity—the God of Israel, now the God of the Christians—and not to the gods of Rome.

Clement (circa 180 C.E.) claimed that the real theme of the story of Adam and Eve is moral freedom and responsibility. Its point was to show that we are responsible for the choices we freely make—good or evil.[1] In contrast, radical Christians felt that the sin of Adam and Eve was sexual—that the fruit of the Tree of Knowledge of Good and Evil conveyed, above all, carnal knowledge. Clement denounced all such views. Sexual intercourse, he stated, was not sinful, but part of God's original and good creation.[2] Since men and women were created for this purpose, Adam's action cannot be construed as carnal knowledge.

Gregory of Nyssa (circa 335–75 C.E.) spoke for the whole tradition when he said, "The soul directly reveals its royal and excellent quality in that . . . it is governed and ruled autonomously by its own free will."[3] Justin and Clement stated the same idea previously: Adam's action did not encroach upon our individual freedom; every person is free to choose good or evil.

Many Christian fathers believed that the theory of "original sin" repudiated the twin foundations of the Christian faith: the goodness of God's creations and the freedom of human will. The whole point of the Adam story, most Christians assumed, was to warn everyone who heard it *not* to misuse that divinely given capacity for free choice. In the Sermon on the Mount, Jesus demanded that his followers control their own natures by taking *moral responsibility* for their acts and mastering such *instinctual* responses as anger and sexual desire (Matthew 5, 21, 27–28).

During the fourth century, certain Christians, influenced by Greek science and philosophy, argued that human desire and will in themselves have no effect on natural events—that humanity neither brought death upon itself, nor could it, by an act of will, overcome death; death was in the nature of things, despite the clear statement to the contrary in Genesis. (Julian claimed that death in the Adam story represented spiritual death.[4])

It was Augustine (circa 354–430 C.E.), using persuasive arguments that suited the church in relation to the sociopolitical climate of the time, who caused the church to adopt his arguments as the official church view. Augustine regarded the current state of nature as punishment. He insisted that Adam's sin brought upon us universal corruption, that is, the sin corrupted the whole of nature. Man cannot choose not to sin. Augustine, who lived after the age of Constantine, viewed the story as one of human bondage—that all of humankind and nature was fallen and that the human will was incorrigibly corrupt. (It is strange that the choice made by the first man and woman could change nature itself, which was created by God prior to their action.) Augustine claimed that the reason Adam's sin deprived Adam's progeny of the freedom to choose not to sin was because he regarded Adam as a corporate personality.

The Christian doctrine of original sin has been restated by modern Christian scientists as follows:

> Man is the offspring of a long line of nonhuman ancestors and therefore is endowed with the same basic desires which his animal brethren possess. These desires—if unchecked—can lead to sins of all kinds. All sins based on greed, or springing from sexual desires, all sins arising from man's drive for power and domination over other human beings—these are the basic drives which he has inherited from millions of years of animal ancestors. In other words, original sin comes in whether we like it or not.*

The viewpoint expressed above is quite general in our society today, that man is fundamentally and primarily an animal and cannot get away from his origin. This bears examination. Animals are not greedy—humans may be. All animals do not possess a drive for power and domination. Why ascribe man's inheritance

---

*Material paraphrased from a personal letter to me dated August 3, 1964, from Dr. William Albright, the late eminent archaeologist.

only to those animals that possess them? Greed and drive for power and domination are sinful only because of the intent and motivation by man to advance his selfish purposes and gain. One cannot ascribe intent to animals; they simply try to exist by instinct, as is their nature. Our sin is, therefore, not something we inherited from our ancestors but is due to a factor in man that is lacking in animals.

Are there sins springing from "sexual desires"? We would not be here without such desires. True, an obsessive drive for sex may be considered as sinful, but no more so than a woman's excessive obsession with beauty or a man's excessive obsession with food. All these may lead to unfortunate "happenings." The sinful part is in the excessive obsession, not natural desires. If anything, animals are not obsessed with sex; they merely obey their natural desires as God has created them to function. Again, the sinfulness is in man's excessive preoccupation with what is supposedly a natural, inherited factor.

If we are concerned mainly with basic desires inherited from animals as a scientific view of man, where does the good impulse in man come from? If the existence of man is simply a result of the evolutionary process, on what basis can we ascribe reason, inalienable rights of life, freedom, and equality, and furthermore, what motivation would man have to act responsibly and morally?

Early generations of Jews and Christians saw in Genesis the affirmation of human freedom to choose *good* or *evil*. However, Genesis 2–4 does not affirm the human freedom to choose good or evil, but only the *knowledge of the difference between good and evil*. Without such knowledge, man would not be able to choose good or evil. This knowledge is a prerequisite for choosing one in preference to the other. Adam, therefore, did not sin—that is, he did not choose evil over good; he only chose to know the difference between the two.

Christianity conceives the idea of redemption in a manner that transfers activity from man to God. Judaism strictly differentiates between the purification of oneself, an obligation that is laid upon man, and eventual redemption through man's actions, which is then granted by God. The reliance on divine intervention, or on the arrival of the Messiah, is not permitted in Jewish law. A basic principle of Jewish law is that Jews are masters of their own fate and that reliance on divine intervention is inappropriate and halakhically prohibited. Halakhic decisors resist the invocation of any divine interference, even in disputes relating to Jewish law, and certainly not in factual disputes subject to empirical and historical resolution.[5] Rather, Judaism teaches, encourages, and even mandates self-help in the face of adverse conditions.

The realm of human nature is conceived in traditional rabbinic thought as coming under man's conscious control. He is free to structure the human realm in accordance with his intellectually informed and deliberate choice.

Notes

1. Elaine Pagels, *Adam, Eve and the Serpent* (New York: Random House, 1988), p. xxiii.
2. Ibid., p. 27.
3. Ibid., p. 73.
4. Ibid., p. 129.
5. See generally Encyclopedia Talmadit 5:1 (Ba'at Kol for the scope of the prohibition of relying on divine intervention). This was taken from Michael Broyde and Emanuel Rackman, "Halacha and the State of Israel," *Midstream*, February/March 1990, p. 13.

Chapter III
Adam's Resolution of the Test—the New Interpretation of the Test of Adam

The Adam story represents the first confrontation between God and man. While the story is a myth, as Louis Jacob says, "The word myth does not mean simply a fairy tale. It implies a grand presentation of an eternal truth which is not diminished even if the event itself did not actually happen."[1] Ahad Ha'Am states: "Every man who leaves a perceptible mark on that life, though he may be a purely imaginary figure, is a real historical force; his existence is a fact of history."[2]

The compilers of the Torah were wise and inspired men, who went through considerable discussion at the time to decide whether to keep the Adam story in the Torah and how to present it. Because it was the first story of the first man in confrontation with his God, the decision to keep it, in the manner presented, illustrated its significance as a lesson for mankind. The compilers were faced with the problem of explaining how the world and man came into being in contrast to the ideas and views of the prevalent pagan world; to show that the human arena is not the playground for the gods of the pagans to play out their drama; to reject the concept that man is a prisoner of fate; and to show that man's conduct is not independent of his God and, finally, that man has a choice in life in relation to good and evil, which constitutes the moral facet of humanity. The redactors of the Torah knew that *yetzer hara* (evil impulse) and *yetzer tov* (good impulse) were an important part of the human condition. Thus the religious genius of the Jew realized that in the first story about man the whole spectrum of the "knowledge of good and evil" had to be introduced.

A reader of this story, the so-called Test of Adam, will immediately sense a turbulence of facts and reason. Many questions cry out for explanation. Some of these questions are:

1. Why was the command stated in the negative? ("Do not . . .")
2. What was the purpose of the command?
3. What is the significance of the tree representing knowledge of both good and evil?
4. Is there a positive lesson to be learned from the story? And there are many others.

God creates man and almost immediately challenges him to a test. Also, the challenge is, "Do not . . ."—a negative approach. Why? God could have easily challenged Adam to "eat this fruit" to determine the degree of Adam's obedience. It would have been much easier for Adam to obey God, especially with the fruit appearing so tempting. A positive act would be evidence of obedience. However, a negative act, that of not eating, would not necessarily amount to disobedience, for one would never know whether the decision was being postponed for a time or the challenge was being disobeyed. The first story of man had to show that the choice presented by God was considered by Adam before he took action. In other words, the action by Adam was to be shown as a definite premeditated choice, and the only definite way of proving his consideration was by an actual positive act of seeming disobedience.

In view of this, one must analyze the thesis stating that the mere disobedience of Adam, the rejection of the voice of de facto authority over the subservient, was a sin and, therefore, he was punished. Here one senses an apparent contradiction. If God gave Adam a free will, it was certainly not sinful to use it, and given free will, man is not subservient but is autonomous in his decision. Indeed, the promise of punishment as a result of a given choice signifies or even demands that man meditate on the order prior to any action. It follows that when considering the choice offered by God to follow the order and have peace of mind or reject it, with the attendant threat of punishment, the factor that determines the choice is of great importance. If not, it would be easy to obey orders by God and, indeed, one doubts that an order would even be given. Therefore, when an order is given, man must consider the alternatives and make a premeditated choice. As a side remark, it may be said that if man engages in this struggle of choice, even for a moment, he cannot claim as an asset complete blind obedience. One would, therefore, contend that blind obedience is really not possible for man and, as a consequence, God does not demand blind obedience. It is of interest to note that nowhere in the Torah concerning this story is the word *sin* mentioned. It is, however, used subsequently in the Cain story.

Why did God set the choice to the first man even before any other human being was born? The answer may be that no extraneous factors were to be introduced to confuse the choice made by Adam. Also, it may be that the question of knowledge of good and evil had to be settled for the human race before any children were to be born. Furthermore, the answer may be that the decision pertained to sex, sex being one important facet in the struggle of good and evil. This premise is supported by the statement "they knew they were naked." However, this statement may be indicative of morality, sexuality being one facet of morality.

The question of *why* God tested Adam is a basic one. The writer has no knowledge of anyone ever posing this question and answering it. And answer one must if the interpretation of the story is to be valid and complete.

Here was man, just created by God in "His Image," the highest living creation of God. "And God saw all that He had made, and found it very good" (1:31). It is strange indeed that immediately afterward God should test Adam. God's omniscience dictates His foreknowledge of Adam's choice. The narratives (2:10–14) discussed in prior pages are indicative of this foreknowledge and support Adam's choice. In view of this, how could God have found His creation very good? The contradiction is readily apparent, and if God knew that Adam would disobey, why test him? Was it so that God would have an excuse for punishment? Of course not. The question, therefore, arises as to the purpose of the command. There were many trees in the garden. The chances of Adam eating from this particular tree were slight, had it not been pointed out to him. By pointing out the tree, God elevated it to a symbol.

Adam became curious; he began to question the reason for the command, and an inner struggle developed within him. Why did God attach such importance to knowledge of good and evil? Why single this out in preference to everything else? A Tree of Life was mentioned, but no prohibition was attached to it. Moreover, Adam reasoned, why should God put this tree in the garden if He did not want man to know the difference between good and evil? If God were testing Adam, the subject of the test could have been more appropriate, specifically in view of the penalty, the Tree of Life and consequently the Tree of Knowledge of Good and Evil need not have been mentioned at all. One may question whether this episode was a test at all. God showed his faith in Adam by having him name the animals. Wasn't testing him totally unnecessary?

The only conclusion from Adam's inner struggle had to be that God actually wanted him to know the fruit of that tree. To reinforce his conclusion, Adam then proceeded to analyze whether eating of the fruit would lead to a contradiction whereby he would have to deny God. To Adam, it was obvious that the choice was with respect to knowledge of good and evil or the realization of what constitutes good and evil and the degrees thereof. To him, there was no question of demonstrating his capacity for good or evil, but rather whether he, and through him mankind, should know the difference and realize its implication. In other words, should man realize the character of his actions and therefore be responsible for them? If man did not know the difference between good and evil, man would never truly sin and yet could perpetrate some terrible acts that, in effect, would be a denial of God. Adam reasoned that God's challenge would imply that obedience to God requires a mind devoid of knowledge of good and evil. This is a contradiction. Adam became convinced, therefore, that the conclusion he reached was, in essence, God's intent and that there was really no alternative but to eat the fruit. The fact that the command was given at the very beginning, without God giving Adam a chance to demonstrate his behavior, only reinforced Adam's conclusion. It showed that God considered this knowledge as a necessary prerequisite to human development. Only on this basis can one explain the timing of this so-called test occurring at the very beginning of man's existence.

Had Adam not reached the conclusion he did, man would not know the meaning of good and evil or have a concept of a moral God, for this requires reason, freedom of choice, and the ability to differentiate right from wrong. Furthermore, Adam's decision elevated man above the animals. Had he chosen not to eat of the fruit, he would have remained as an animal who might do good or evil but does not have a moral concept of his acts.

The first story of the first man thus becomes the lesson that the knowledge of good and evil forms the very basis of man's spiritual and moral behavior. The fruit of the tree becomes the fundamental thread in the life of man and religion. As it is written in the Torah, it is through the very eating of the fruit, knowing the difference between good and evil, that God says, "The man has become like one of us" (3:22). It is seldom that a man with the sense of knowing this difference and becoming committed to it is found among the evil, criminal element of society, and the man of saintly character has the highest sense of right and wrong.

Adam was commanded not to eat the fruit of the Tree of Knowledge of Good and Evil under threat of death. If the tree were the means by which man's moral judgment (or self-determination) was to be acquired, God here must be represented as unwilling for man to rise above the nonmoral level of animals. It may also be claimed that the expulsion was not because Adam *wrongly* acquired the knowledge of good and evil, but because he had come to possess it at all. This knowledge (he became "like one of us") together with the possibility of eating from the Tree of Life and thus obtaining immortality would prevent human life as we know it. Therefore, the expulsion was in order to begin the history of humankind. Thus both of the above arguments cannot be justified.

One other point may be made to show that the Adam story was not really a test but represented a challenge and a choice. "The Tree of Knowledge of Good and Evil" means that the fruit of the tree consisted of both elements. If the story was a "test," there would be no necessity for the tree to represent both good and evil; indeed, it would be more logical if it represented only evil. However, if the intent of the story was to be a lesson for mankind, it would be more logical for both elements to be represented. The fusion of good and evil in one fruit implies that one cannot exist without the other and that every characteristic has a polarity between which there is a whole spectrum of qualities. Man is neither good nor bad, but he is the only creation as a result of Adam's choice that has the possibility of following in the direction of positive polarity. Human life is full of characteristics of inherent polarity—heroism and cowardice, honesty and dishonesty, love and hate, indeed, life and death itself. The punishment in the story was certainty of death, but the certainty of death is the very prime force leading man toward love, compassion, justice—that is, the positive polarity of life that, in the final analysis, leads him closer to God. If man knew he would live forever, would he desire to gravitate toward the positive polarity? (See p. 8 for another explanation of why the threat of death was not actually a threat.)

At this point, reference should be made to the question of sin. In the Torah, God said:

> Let us make man in our image, after our likeness. And God created man in His image, in the image of God He created him.
> —1:26–27

Man is the only creature that has any "image relationship" to God. Therefore, man is immediately elevated above all other creatures in his potential. Thus it is indeed very difficult to view man as being inherently sinful or bad. Furthermore, only man can comprehend the idea of God, has the capacity for "understanding" God, and, indeed, yearns and strives for such understanding. If God imbued man with this higher comprehension, can that intelligence be inherently sinful?

It is the Christian viewpoint that sin entered the world through the action of Adam. However, by advancing the notion that Adam's action was not a sin the author must explain how sin was introduced into the world.

It is logical to say that man comprehends sin only because he has an understanding of good and evil. Without this understanding, the concept of sin would not exist. Man would not be able to evaluate his actions and, therefore, he would not realize whether he sins or not. Man would live in a true moral vacuum. Adam's action resulted in our ability to evaluate ourselves in relation to God. It has nothing to do with the quality of our actions, only with the understanding of our actions. Actually, sin was not introduced by Adam, only the comprehension of what it means. How was sin then introduced? It was not. It was no more introduced as a special characteristic than was any other attribute of man. What was the first sin? Cain's murder of his brother, Abel, may be considered the first sin in the history of mankind, because Cain already knew the difference between good and evil. He knew that killing Abel was an act of murder. Sin in general may be considered as that action that is not based on an examination of good and evil or, in spite of such examination, is consciously directed toward the "wrong" end of polarity.

The problem of the test now resolves itself into the problem: why the punishment? If the story was not a test but merely posed a question for Adam that had to be solved, there should not be any punishment. Let us, therefore, analyze the nature of the punishment.

The punishment for the serpent is not really relevant to our discussion. The punishment for the man promised by God in the injunction not to eat the fruit resulted in a limited life, ending in death. It has been shown that death may not be considered as punishment (see p. 9) inasmuch as it is a prime force for the improvement of mankind in the context of the religio-moral perspective. The other punishment for Eve and Adam was not promised beforehand. It may, therefore, be considered of secondary importance and as an outgrowth of the choice made by Adam. To Eve, God said:

> I will make most severe your pangs in childbearing; in pain shall you bear children. Yet your urge shall be for your husband, and he shall rule over you.
>
> —3:16

The punishment is the suffering of pain in childbearing, and yet the urge of the woman shall be for her husband. God has given man the power to alleviate that pain through modern medicines, which would indicate that perhaps the "punishment" of woman was not intended as a punishment. It should be noted that birth—be it by animals or humans—is a painful experience. Therefore, the question could be asked: if God's intention was to punish Eve, why punish the animals as well? It is interesting to note that God, in creating Eve, put Adam to sleep—an indication of the existence of pain during the act of creation. The question, therefore, one must keep in mind is: if God saw fit to create the second human by an action involving pain, should mere man be able to create life without pain?

To Adam, God said:

> Cursed be the ground because of you; in anguish shall you eat of it all the days of your life. Thorns and thistles shall it bring forth for you, and you shall feed on the grains of the field. By the sweat of your brow shall you get bread to eat, until you return to the ground, for from it you were taken; for dust you are, and to dust you shall return.
>
> —3:17–18

The implied punishment is that the earth will be productive only as a result of hard work, and this will last through a man's life. Work is the punishment. Is it? In the early stages of civilization, earning a living was indeed an extremely hard task. In modern society, the number of hours necessary to earn a living decreases with time, allowing for some idleness. But if idleness were the dominant factor in everyone's life, what would be the state of society? It is not pleasant to contemplate. For most people, too much leisure time poses problems with which they cannot cope. They have not reached the adequate state of intellectual, psychological, and moral development one needs for the proper use of leisure time. Again, it seems, therefore, that the punishment was not really a punishment, but a pathway for the development of society along which one may learn the use of leisure.

Furthermore, when man works hard in achieving a goal, the satisfaction in achievement is great. It is, indeed, greater when man participates in the work of creation, as one does when he grows food in what was promised to be a hostile ground. Is this punishment, when one participates and rejoices in the very process of creation for which we revere God?

We may ask why didn't Adam eat of the Tree of Life before he "disobeyed" God and thus circumvent the "punishment"? If he intended to disobey God, he would have prevented the promised consequences. The answer suggests that Adam believed that he was acting in accordance with God's intention. There is another possible interpretation. The Torah is referred to as the Tree of Life. If, as some commentators on the Torah claim, the Tree of Knowledge of Good and Evil enveloped the Tree of Life, it is reasonable to assume that the knowledge of good and evil was a necessary prerequisite to receiving the Torah later. The Torah could not have been made available to a single individual. The Torah has to be available to a whole nation, being in a major way a "political" document, for it to have a direct influence on the people and, through them, on the world at large. It is in this sense that the Jewish people are called witnesses of God and bear a mission to the world.

In conclusion, the thesis submits that Adam acquired a spiritual and moral facet by his action in response to his considered judgment of the intent of God's command. As such, the story of Adam may be considered part and parcel of the story of creation. Genesis 2:2–3 reads:

> The heaven and the earth were finished, and all their array. And on the seventh day, God finished the work which He had been doing, and He ceased on the seventh day from all the work which He had done. And God blessed the seventh day.

The question arises: what was the work God had been doing that He finished on the seventh day? It is the writer's contention that the Test of Adam occurred on the seventh day. There is nothing in Genesis to contradict this suggestion, and, indeed, the test follows chronologically the six days of creation. In six days God created the physical world. A physical world is not a complete world, however. Therefore, on the seventh day, God concerned himself with the moral and spiritual, the final and crowning act of creation. In this task man was asked to participate. God could have created man with "perfect" spiritual and moral insight. However, man was created deliberately as a physical being only so that God could make man a partner in the greatest creation. In this way, the spiritual and moral values could be emphasized for mankind. The negative command to Adam now attains additional significance, and the question of the purpose of the test is thus answered.

Judah Halevi maintains that Adam was perfect in body and mind. Adam was endowed with the "divine power" (*ha-ko'ah he-Elohi*)—that special faculty that, according to Halevi, enables man to achieve communion with God. (Why, then, did Adam disobey God?[3])

Unlike Halevi, Maimonides believed that communion can be achieved through the development of the intellect and that no special faculty is necessary. Adam, as a result of the test, began to acquire practical rather than theoretical knowledge, a knowledge of values rather than facts (truth and falsehood). For Maimonides, practical wisdom is inferior to theoretical wisdom and, therefore, the activation of Adam's practical wisdom at the expense of his theoretical reason was a punishment. If Adam were created with a perfect intellect, why did he succumb to the desire for practical wisdom? Furthermore, intellect does not signify moral behavior, which is a most important fact of life. Reason cannot provide a reason to be reasonable.

Notes

1. Louis Jacob, "Faith and Reason," *Jewish Heritage*, Spring 1963, p. 6.
2. Ahad Ha'Am, in selected essays, *Moses* (Philadelphia: Jewish Publication Society, 1912), p. 307.
3. Kuzari 1:95, abridged ed. with introduction and commentary by Isaac Heineman (New York: East and West Library, 1948).

Chapter IV
Adam's Choice as the Paradigm of Responsible Freedom

The narratives in Genesis that deal archetypically with man, e.g., those of Adam and the Tree of Knowledge of Good and Evil, Cain and Abel, etc., are intended to reveal something *essential* for our understanding of man, something of the *essence* of the human situation—something that holds for all men at all times. The Christian emphasis on the Adam narrative has been with the "Fall of Man" and the need for a redemption that he cannot effect on his own, i.e., the need for *mediatorship*.

What is offered here is an understanding of the narrative that emphasizes the positiveness of Adam's choice—the first act of choosing. This first act archetypically reveals a positive dimension of man and his relationship with God and that subsequent biblical narratives can be read as a *progression of this dimension*. Thus, instead of emphasizing original sin and the need for mediating redemption, the Adam narrative reveals an original choice that enables man to *rise* in partnership with God. Schematically, this can be represented as follows:

Christian interpretation: Choice = fall requiring mediatorship

My interpretation: Choice = elevation leading to partnership in which justice and compassion among fellowmen are important

Reason is a major reflection of the image relationship between man and God. An ignorant man cannot conceive of a moral God. A person with little ability to think may be religious in the sense of blindly following prescribed church injunctions, but he has little comprehension of the meaning of the relationship to make it a part of him. A person of higher intellect and rational insight is capable of having a more highly developed concept of God. It is reason that makes one seek meaning in life and its mystery.

In Genesis 1:26, man was created in the image of God, an image that represents reason and free will, among other faculties. Reason then becomes a natural characteristic of man. Thus reason is a necessary, though not sufficient, condition for religious understanding and commitment. The validity of any religious concept that contradicts reason must be suspect because it implies a denial of the image of God and thus cuts the link between man and God. If God created man with the powers of reason, the use of reason cannot be irreligious. It follows that it is a religious obligation for man to seek religious truth by rational means.

The resolution of the Test of Adam should be considered as having been based on man's use of reason. The very offer of a choice by God, the way it was presented and involving as it did many inconsistencies and unreasonable punishment, was designed so that Adam should question the purpose of the choice and go through a careful analysis to arrive at a logical resolution of the choice.

Nature and natural laws were completed as far as animals were concerned when Adam and Eve became a reality. Nature, however, was not completed as far as man was concerned merely by the physical creation of Adam and Eve. Human nature could only be completed by an *act* of Adam and Eve. That God commanded Adam and not any of the other animals implies that the other animals were designed to follow their instincts, while man had the choice and possibility of creating his own existential condition. Having been given reason, Adam had to judge even God's commandment by means of rational inquiry. The story in this sense represented the philosophical first thing, in the *obvious absence of convention and law* and in view of its being the first choice and the first act by man. Adam's choice represented the actualization of the human possibility, the partnership of ethical relations.

One lesson from the Adam test was that God implied that man was free to choose and, therefore, must remain free to do so. Indeed, atonement by man suggests a different choice from the one before. Adam was born to choose between two alternatives—a sort of two-dimensional freedom.

In choosing the knowledge of good and evil, Adam added a new dimension to freedom. This dimension of freedom imposes restraints on itself for the sake of true freedom (responsible freedom) as opposed to absolute freedom. This comes about only through the acceptance of the responsibility of existence or Godman partnership, which gives birth to the *responsible element* of freedom. Without this, man is free to be evil; with this, man is not free to be evil. Without this, man is free to master others; with this, man is free to master himself. After the Adam test, man's freedom acquired a self-imposed responsible element, which is a necessary condition for partnership with God.

Choice is the central religious issue for man, because the meaning of a man's life is determined by his choices; a nonchoice is also choice—of indifference. Man always chooses what his qualitative existence will be, what he will become. Through the process of choice, man is self-determining; if man opts for partnership with God, man adds his share toward the redemption of the world.

Adam faced a choice that may be stated as follows:

1. *To follow God's command and refrain from partaking of the fruit of knowledge of good and evil.* In this case, man would not know the difference between good and evil and, therefore, would not be able to evaluate his actions. *Man would live in a moral vacuum.* It would be a world without the concept of a moral God, for this requires not only the reason but also the ability to differentiate right from wrong.
2. *To partake of the fruit and thus become aware of the difference between good and evil.* In this case, man would liberate himself from the animal and elevate himself to a higher level of existence. This would permit man to become responsible for his own moral situation.

Adam could lead a simple, meaningless existence devoid of values of behavior, standards of commitment, and a sense of fulfillment, or he could create his own existential situation—that is, become aware of himself as an "I" (an existentialist subject) who must bear alone the responsibility for his own situation. The Adam story dramatizes the dreadful freedom of our choices. The threat of death for partaking of the fruit of the tree further introduced the ultimate despair and absurdity of existence. The choice was between a meaningless existence or an authentic existence ending in the nothingness of death. Adam decided, as each one of us would have and could have done no less, that a meaningful existence committed to the knowledge of good and evil was preferred to a meaningless existence, even though it entails its own finite end.

Adam's action of becoming aware of himself as an individual, as an "I," and thus assuming the responsibility for himself leads to the awareness that the other person is also potentially an "I." The existential "I," however, cannot live within the limit of unidimensional (self)responsibility. The world cannot exist on this basis. I do not agree with Sartre that when a man chooses for his own good, it is necessarily good for everybody. This is true only when man chooses on the basis of partnership with God. The responsibility must be extended to interrelate the "I's."

Thus we are led to a community of "I's," a peoplehood of covenantal responsibility and partnership with God. This is different from a community of faith only. It is an active community of people who see themselves in a unique relationship with God by their free, autonymous choices of accepting God's assignment of the moral realm to man. Adam's choice did not alienate him from God; he came closer to God. As it is said, "he became like one of us" (3:22).

The Adam story ties together the partnership with God with the finiteness of man. Can this be otherwise? Would man want to choose responsibility of existence if he knew he was immortal? *God made the condition of finitude accompany the choice for a meaningful existence as a partner of God.* If one rejects the choice of God, he is in a finite condition without compensatory, meaningful value. However, by an autonomous choice of partnership in which man lives in harmony with God's intent, the finite condition is ameliorated, because man thereby gives meaning to his finite existence. Man's ontological doubt is, therefore, erased. In support of this, I cite the statement of God in Genesis 3:22 as stated previously. Man is now ready to act out his partnership role in conformity with God's intent.

As a partner of God, man has faith in himself to make a proper choice in each situation as a result of his own analysis and in conformity with the assumed hypothesis. Having made the choice, man can be expected to live in accordance with it, for it arose out of his own deep convictions and intellectual resolve. Kant pointed out that no command from outside of the individual can stand strictly as an ethical command unless it is also, at the same time, *self-imposed.*

The Adam story reveals God as the challenger to all people. All mankind is challenged by God to accept the knowledge of good and evil and thus to assume the responsibility for the moral condition of this world. In accepting this challenge, man actualizes God's intent. Man continues the work of creation, to fulfill the unfulfilled, to complete the incomplete, to humanize the inhuman, to actualize the potential, to create light in darkness, to do good and eliminate evil, and to become responsibly committed and eliminate indifference. Man does this by the recognition of the rights of others, self-discipline, intellect, justice, love, mercy, openness, responsiveness, and responsibleness.

In the choice presented to Adam, God appears as a challenger to man, which speaks of God's immanence. The immanent God challenges man to accept the responsibility of existence and thus become a partner of God. When man accepts the challenge of God, God is manifested in the daily reality of life. When man rejects the responsibility of partnership, he denies his own humanity and God.

The outlook of our age has increasingly become characterized by secularity. Secularity is often taken to mean the attitude of modern science and of this worldly concern. However, secularity represents a more rigid attitude that holds that *only* through science is any trustworthy knowledge to be obtained and that *only* the tangible and human affairs of this world are worthy of attention.

The secular and the worldly are opposed to what is called "other worldly." The secularist, then, is the man who affirms the temporal character of existence. Moreover, he is concerned with the tasks of this world, which are surely vast: peace, justice, poverty, pollution, education, population control, and a thousand other matters that cry out for his efforts. However, these are the problems that have been *caused by man,* not by God.

The secular man is the autonomous man. Since there is no higher being than man himself, he must originate his own values, set his own standards, and create the means for his own salvation. He cannot look for any support beyond himself. The secularist finds a certain exhilaration in his autonomy, a challenge that generates effort and energy.

The secularist finds that religion stands in the way of autonomous human freedom and responsibility. To the secularist, God appears to be the rival of man. We are told that man cannot really be free to order this world and build a better future unless God is deposed and man assumes complete responsibility. Nonetheless, the fact that there is a world rather than just nothing, an ordered and structured world rather than chaos, and this world brought forth spiritual and personal beings makes the complete deposition of God a most improbable thesis.

In secular language, freedom and responsibility belong to every human existent so that he cannot submit himself to another human being without losing his authentic being. Consequently, there are an unlimited number of values and goals, especially since there is no direction provided for these. There are times (perhaps in the lives of all of us) when we are jolted out of "everyday" and compelled to ask questions about the wider context of human life that range far afield. Since the Holocaust during World War II, or precisely because of it, intelligent people are still asking about issues of ultimate value. The result of not having limits on values is that men in the age of technology have made many advances in controlling the physical world and destiny without accepting the responsibility of controlling such world crises as pollution, ecological destruction, and war.

Nowadays theology has to be practiced in a secularized world. If the theologian cannot avoid the responsibility of speaking of God, it is equally true that he cannot avoid the responsibility of addressing himself to his own world and speaking the language of his time.

Contemporary theology is in search of synthesis between God and secularity. It is my claim that the story of creation and the Adam story represent the essence of secularity. Man, in being assigned dominion over this world (1:28) and in accepting the divine challenge to assume the partnership with God (the Adam test), expresses his active commitment to this world. Every human arena becomes man's responsibility, and every act becomes a spiritual expression of his role as God's partner.

God does not intervene in human history or solve problems for man. However, every activity of man has a dimension of sacredness if it is approached on the basis of partnership with God. With any other approach, the secular becomes "profane." With man a partner of God, life in its totality is one continuous spiritual experience and commitment. As such, the secular has no existence of its own; it exists only in the form of potentiality, which man's actions will determine as profane or sacred. Human action gives the secular the form of existence. Man as the partner of God indeed gives every act a spiritual dimension.

The meaning of the Adam test is not as a defense for the humanistic approach to life. Simply stated, the humanistic approach is based on the premise that since all problems arise from man's action, the solution is also human in character. In this presentation, God is not present, so man's initiative and responsibility are preserved. The partner of God also sees the solutions of problems in the human domain, so long as they are viewed in the light of partnership. The direction of the solution is certainly different in the two approaches. In the humanistic approach, man is the measurer of his own values, limited only by a legal system imposed by society. The partner of God approaches the solution from the viewpoint of inalienable rights and responsible freedom, the assignment of this world to man, and his acceptance of it. The partner is not the measurer of his own values. God is present in every deliberation and solution of problems. It is also significant that the Noahide laws as well as six of the commandments apply to man-to-man relationships.

Radical theology sees God and man as competitors, even enemies. The victor is either God or man. Man has come of age, which necessarily requires complete freedom. But man cannot be free until he kills the last God. Man is free and in freedom he can now accept responsibility for his life. However, without the responsible element of freedom, he can either create or destroy, liberate or enslave. Man becomes the supreme being. He deifies himself by setting his own standards and becoming his own measurer. His responsibility is only to himself.

That anyone can advocate such a view after Auschwitz is beyond understanding. Tolstoy's view of the world is certainly more appropriate—without God, anything is possible. At Auschwitz, man certainly proved this. In the Christian churches, the Christian God was indeed dead. The Christians killed Him: in Germany, among her allies, in the occupied countries—in fact, in the world representing the tradition of Western "civilization." For a period of two thousand years the God of Christian love became a perverted source of persecution, hate, pogroms, and murder. In the Holocaust, the Christian God was indeed killed by his own flock.

Chapter V
The Akedah: A Test of Abraham as a Partner of God

Many volumes have been written on the thought-provoking story of the Akedah. Generally, this story has been considered a test to determine the degree of Abraham's obedience. However, this position cannot withstand critical analysis because of the many questions and contradictions that surface under thorough scrutiny. A discussion of these questions and an attempt at resolving the contradictions lead to a more logical, consistent interpretation of this dramatic story. The new interpretation eliminates the contradictions and does not disturb our sense of morality of God's "demand" of human sacrifice.

The Akedah story should not be considered as an isolated event. Rather, the story is to be seen as part of an ongoing evolving process in which Abraham develops the concepts of God and undergoes spiritual transformation. This process, an outgrowth of the continual encounters between God and Abraham, is an inherently necessary prerequisite for the resolution of the Akedah problem. The introduction by God of the Akedah, therefore, could not have come earlier.

The saga of Abraham begins with a command by God: "Go forth from your native land and from your father's house to the land that I will show you" (12:1). This is followed immediately by God making a promise to Abraham to bless him and to make of him a great nation. Abraham saw this command as an order to continue the journey his father had started from his native land, Ur, to the land of Canaan, but which was interrupted at Haran by his father.

This is confirmed by the destination stated in the following verse (12:5): "They set out for the land of Canaan," even though the name of the place is not mentioned in the command. God later confirms the continuity of the journey verbally (15:7): "I am the Lord who brought you out from Ur of the Chaldeans to give you this land as a possession." The promise of reward and blessing was an additional inducement to do as ordered.

Abraham lived in a pagan world, where people believed in many gods. God, in giving the command to Abraham to go forth from his native land, made Abraham realize that this God was different from the pagan gods, which were local in character and confined to a territory beyond which their authority ceased. Abraham's God would be with him wherever he went—the beginning of the concept of a universal God. At this stage, no sacrificial offering was asked of Abraham. Instead, he was given safe passage. This was completely contrary to the usual beliefs and customs practiced within Abraham's cultural environment, which called for sacrificial offerings to various pagan gods in order to ensure one's safety.

Besides the order to leave his father's house and "go to the land I will show you," nothing else is required of Abraham. Abraham appears as the *silent, passive beneficiary* of God's promises and blessings. This relationship continues in Genesis 12:2, 12:7, and 13:14–17.

Abraham believed God to be the Creator of the world, as stated in Genesis 14:22: "Abram said to the King of Sodom, 'I swear to the Lord Most High, Creator of heaven and earth.'" Abraham's perception of God is further evolved in his recognition of God as a God of mercy. Abraham complains to God about being childless, and God responds with a promise that he will have an heir of his own.

Abraham is no longer the silent party. In response to God's statement (15:7): "I am the Lord who brought you out from Ur . . . to give you this land as a possession," Abraham continues the dialogue (15:8): "O Lord God, how shall I know that I am to possess it?" Abraham is no longer satisfied with general, indefinite promises but demands specific information. Nevertheless, Abraham is still the passive, though not silent, recipient of God's promises. No obligation of any type is required of him.

Abraham's concept of God is further developed when God says to him (17:1), "Walk in My ways and be blameless." Abraham's actions henceforth should be in conformity with his understanding of God's ways. For the first time, he is called upon to assume an obligation. Immediately following God's charge to Abraham to assume an active role, God says (17:2): "I will establish My covenant between Me and you . . . " For the first time, the word *covenant*[1] is mentioned directly to Abraham and it follows immediately the call for an active role requiring an obligation and participation on his part.

As part and parcel of the covenant, God changes Abram's name to Abraham (17:5). In the ancient Near Eastern world, a name was not merely a means of identification. The name of a man was intimately involved in the very essence of his being, reflecting his personality. A new name meant a corresponding change in destiny. Linking the covenant containing the corresponding obligation of Abraham with the change of name was, therefore, very significant. Abraham now assumes a more elevated relationship with God. *He is an active participant with a new destiny*. Abraham's obligation in fulfilling the covenant with God was not only to circumcise himself, but to make sure that everyone in his household, including the bought slaves (17:12), was circumcised. Abraham thus had to *assume responsibility for others* as well as for himself.

Abraham was next shown that he was expected to know what is just and right and to act accordingly. God says (18:19):

"For I have singled him out, that he may instruct his children and his posterity to keep the ways of the Lord by doing what is just and right, in order that the Lord may bring about for Abraham what He has promised him." It is a clear statement that man's responsibility to do what is just and right is not only a precondition to the fulfillment of God's promise, but also a necessary ingredient in Abraham's transformation to enable him to justify the questions he raises in his next encounter with God.

The narrative of Sodom and Gomorrah follows, and Abraham, having become aware of his responsibility to "do what is right and just," raises the questions to God: "Will you sweep away the innocent along with the guilty?" (18:23) and "Shall not the Judge of all the earth deal justly?" (18:25). For the first time, Abraham raises the issue of justice and morality. The questions by Abraham imply that man's moral responsibility extends even to the point of questioning God. By posing the questions repeatedly, and God's answering patiently, Abraham showed that the belief in God does not necessitate blind faith or the surrender of logic. Indeed, it implies that even God's command, when contrary to man's sense of justice and morality, should be questioned repeatedly, because God Himself is subject to the same requirement of justice and morality that He demands of man. It is to be noted that in Talmud Baba Metsia 59b, Rabbi Joshua clearly states that God, too, is subject to the Torah, which He cannot alter in any manner. Abraham has now evolved into an active participant and covenantal partner of God, responsible to discharge his obligation in the sphere of justice and morality.

The transformation of Abraham from a passive recipient of God's promise into an active participant and partner of God in the sphere of justice and morality sets the stage for the resolution of the problem of child sacrifice. Without this transformation and the evolving concepts of God, the problem could not be resolved, and therefore the Akedah was not introduced until this stage. For that reason, God delayed Isaac's birth until Abraham's transformation was complete, despite His promise of an heir made long before the birth. The expulsion of Ishmael before the Akedah was also necessary to reduce the complexity of the situation. Without Ishmael, Isaac was an "only" son (i.e., the only one left with Abraham)—which made the test all the more poignant. No extraneous issues were to be introduced into the drama.

We now come to the "test" of Abraham. We may ask what its purpose was? God's challenge is for the benefit of the person being tested. Since this world is to serve as the medium for human free-willed performance, when God puts man to a challenge it is in order to permit him to translate potential into reality.

Since child sacrifice was a common practice within the cultural setting of Abraham's environment, the command by God at first did not seem to be of an outrageous nature to Abraham. However, it soon appeared to him that something was amiss. The demand by God to sacrifice Isaac presented Abraham with a dilemma. Why and for what purpose did God require the sacrifice of Abraham's son? Spiritual confusion, love of God, love of his son, his understanding of God as one of justice, and mercy and as the Creator of life must have surely torn at his heart. Abraham decided that an agonizing analysis was required for him to understand.[2] Hamlet's question "to be or not to be" pales beside Abraham's dilemma, "to slay or not to slay." He considered that the resolution of this question involved much more than simple obedience to God. He reasoned that the purpose of the command was for him to develop a deeper understanding of God and of his relationship to Him, because it was important not only to Abraham and Isaac, but to the future of Abraham's dream of a new true religion, of a new society, and of a new world with the vision of one God. The future itself was at stake. Abraham knew that he must answer the question and resolve the conflicts before the final act in this intense drama was played out by him.

Doing otherwise would be an irresponsible act on his part, not worthy of a covenantal responsibility.

The generally accepted interpretation of the Akedah claims that God tested Abraham's faith. However, Abraham had displayed faith before when the order for him to go forth from his father's house was accompanied by a promise that he was to become the progenitor of a great nation. Since this was not a promise that could possibly be fulfilled in his lifetime, it was something that had to be accepted on faith. In view of the fact that Sarah was barren, Abraham's faith must really have been taxed. Some rabbis claim that the test was to enable God to be sure that He had chosen the right man for the task of pioneering the new way in which God wanted man to walk. Was Abraham the right man for the task? If God chose Abraham, there was no question that he was the right man. Otherwise, the implication would be that God could err in His judgment. There can be no question that the test was not necessary from the point of view of God. (Rambam 22:1 states: "All trials in the Torah are for the benefit of the one being tested.") The issue of child sacrifice had to be resolved. The current interpretation of the test, which portrays Abraham as not willing to withhold his only beloved son from God as a matter of faith only, does not resolve the problem of child sacrifice. Indeed, the desire to emulate Abraham in his faith may be the reason child sacrifice surfaced several times in ancient Israel.

If Abraham went through the process of sacrificing Isaac without questioning the command, which is a requirement of the current interpretation, can we really definitely state that Abraham's action was solely due to his faith in God? After all, *God's command was entirely compatible with the prevalent custom of child sacrifice. Which factor, then, was responsible for Abraham's actions?* Why should God demand that Abraham follow a pagan custom? We can say that Abraham did not follow the command blindly. When he received the order to sacrifice his son, he did not openly argue with God as he did at the time of the destruction of Sodom and Gomorrah. At that time, he argued, "Will You sweep away the righteous along with the guilty?" (18:23). One would expect Abraham to argue with God again, especially since it involved his son. Why did he not? In the Sodom and Gomorrah story, Abraham argues for nameless people. In this case, he would have to argue for someone close to him. Therefore, the argument could be viewed as being selfish in motivation. Thus he did not openly argue with God. However, silence does not suggest that the arguments were not taking place in his mind. Logic, fatherly love, and concern would require that Abraham subject the demand to a critical review at this moment of anguish. I suggest that the journey of three days was precisely to provide sufficient time for Abraham to think about the problem. God could have picked a place closer than Moriah, but the story had to show that there was sufficient time for Abraham to think about the impending action at the end of this journey of anguish and resolve the problem he faced. After three days of what surely must have been intense meditation, Abraham resolved the problem and reached a conclusion. He understood and knew what he had to do. Let us now go through what Abraham may have reasoned to come to his decision.

Being of a critical nature, as attested by the questions about Sodom and Gomorrah, and having become an active participant with and partner of God in this world, Abraham became aware of several contradictions in the situation. Having already asserted the right to question God on justice, Abraham subjected the demand of a sacrifice of a human life to a searching scrutiny and analysis. How could God, having created man in His image, demand the sacrifice of His creation? Having already established the concept of a just God, Abraham must have questioned whether the demand was compatible with this concept. After all, Isaac was innocent. If God were testing Abraham, why involve the life of another person? Most important, it was Isaac's life that was demanded, the very life that God in His mercy had given to Abraham and Sarah. Would God play such tricks on Abraham? Even if God did entertain critical thoughts of this type, His ultimate test represented a contradiction. Hadn't God promised Abraham that He would make his descendants a great nation through Isaac? If Isaac were sacrificed, there would be no descendants. Also, didn't God say, "You shall name him Isaac, and I will maintain My covenant with him as an everlasting covenant" (17:19)? As a test, therefore, it would have been more logical for God to demand Abraham's own life so that God's promise could not be questioned by him. Furthermore, if Abraham went through with the sacrifice, he would be negating God's promise. This was the dilemma—*to follow God's command and thus negate God's promise or not go through with God's command and thereby deny God and His authority.* For three days the struggle continued in Abraham's mind.

How was Abraham to reconcile the two contradictory responses? If Abraham were to sacrifice Isaac, it would suggest that man can negate God's promise, or that God Himself can break an unconditional promise by a subsequent command contradictory to His former promise. This would result in a totally unacceptable theological situation.

Abraham concluded that since God's promise preceded the command to sacrifice Isaac and was made *unconditionally,* Abraham just could not negate the promise by any act of his own. Furthermore, Abraham concluded that the contradictions[3] were deliberately introduced as a part of the command. In so doing, God purposefully called Abraham's attention to the prevalent custom of child sacrifice in pagan culture. Because the evolving concepts of God by Abraham were different from those of the pagan environment, it seemed to him that in the crucial matter of human sacrifice, the true God would also differ from the pagan gods. However, *the only alternative available was the total rejection of the custom,* and thus he concluded that he must not sacrifice Isaac. This decision was fully in accord with Abraham's newly evolved concepts and understanding of his God as one of mercy, justice, righteousness, and love. His God could not require human sacrifice, for if He did, He would be contradicting Himself. Human sacrifice was characteristic of the gods of the people surrounding Abraham, not the one he believed in.

Abraham's conclusion was the result of a logical analysis in his role as a partner of God. However, Abraham had to verify the correctness of his decision. He could do this only by *testing God in the demand of the Akedah*! Therefore, Abraham decided to go through the motions of the process of sacrifice. According to his conclusion, the true God had no choice but to stop him from the actual sacrifice. If God would not prevent the sacrifice, Abraham would abort the act himself, because, for one thing, his God could not be associated with broken promises, injustice, immorality, and contradictory concepts. Man could not relate to such a God, because then man would never know what was demanded of him. For another, Abraham would consider the demand as ultimately originating from pagan culture and, therefore, null and void. This conclusion is in accord with the Torah text. The test begins with a command by Elohim (22:1), a generic term for God or gods. But at the end of the test, at the point of Akedah, the Torah text (22:11) refers to *Adonai*. It is He who stays Abraham's hand. Adonai represents the mature concept of the God of Abraham, which he developed as a result of his spiritual encounters with Him and man's relationship to Him.

The term *tested*, instead of referring to Abraham's faith, must apply to his ability to act as a partner of God to resolve the problem by harmonizing the contradictions of faith, logic, and knowledge of God without doing violence to any of them. Abraham showed that he was capable of acting as a partner of God and that the essence of Judaism was fully developed within him. The fact that after the Akedah there is no other encounter between God and Abraham supports this thesis.

Why didn't Abraham tell his wife, Sarah, and his son, Isaac, of the divine command before leaving on the fateful journey? Saying that he wanted to spare Sarah the pain of the impending event would not be justified by the facts. (Note that this is precisely what the Midrash maintains.) The shock she would endure on learning of the sacrifice after the event would be much worse because it would be compounded by the resentment she would have for Abraham for his failure to tell her. After all, Isaac was her only son, but Abraham had another son. Sarah had the right to know. Why, then, did Abraham keep silent? Also, why not inform Isaac as well? If, as we are told, the purpose of the test was to determine the degree of Abraham's obedience so that God would be sure He had selected the right man for a most important task, why not also demand the same obedience from Isaac, who was destined to continue the new tradition and precepts according to God's own statements of purpose? Otherwise, Isaac appears simply as an innocent victim. This is contrary to the concept of a just God.

Abraham did not tell Sarah or Isaac because he only knew the question, "Why the demand for the sacrifice?," and not the answer. The debate within him had just begun. He would tell them only if he had the answer. Abraham decided that the struggle within him had to remain in anguished silence to reach the correct resolution of the ultimate problem of God, life, death, and child sacrifice. By telling Sarah and Isaac, Abraham would subject himself to intense pressures. Desperate attempts would be made to convince him of the folly of the unjust demand. No, Abraham, as the founder of a new religion, must resolve the basic fundamental problems without interference or influence of external pressures. Sarah and Isaac would beg God for mercy and would ask Abraham to do likewise, for after all, isn't God a God of mercy? The request for mercy, the request to God to withdraw His demand, would not resolve the issue of child sacrifice that God, by making an issue of it, evidently wanted to be solved. The silent torment accompanying the resolution was the only answer, as all deeply religious problems require. This explains the problem posed by Abraham's silence before leaving on the journey.

Abraham's conclusion that the sacrifice of Isaac would not be consummated clearly answers several embarrassing questions. Why did Abraham say to his two servants, "You stay here with the ass. The boy and I will go up there; we will worship and we will return to you" (22:5)? If Abraham were acting on the basis of blind faith, he could not and would not have said "we." However, if he had already reached the conclusion that either he or God would prevent the actual sacrifice, Abraham was telling the truth in saying, "We will return." Similarly, he was telling the truth when he said to Isaac, "God will provide the lamb for his burnt offering." For Abraham it was essential that Isaac should live so that God's promised covenant ("And I will maintain My covenant with him as an everlasting covenant for his offspring to come") should not be nullified.

It is logical to assume that after the "test," Abraham explained to Isaac about the demand of God. Abraham assured his son that he had no intention of slaying him, even if God had not stayed his hand, because the true God did not demand human sacrifices. Isaac, however, must have been very upset.

Having been exposed to infinite anguish and fear, Isaac did not wish to return with his father. Abraham, therefore, came back alone. To quote: "Abraham then returned to his servants" ((22:19). It may be argued that this does not necessarily mean that Abraham returned alone. After all, at the beginning of the Akedah we are told that "he set out for the place of which God had told him" (22:3), even though Isaac and the two servants were with him. However, in this case, we are specifically informed in the same verse that Abraham was not alone. This is not the case in 22:19. Furthermore, at the beginning of the Akedah story, Abraham is at the center of the whole drama. The emphasis must be on him and his actions; hence, "he set out." After the Akedah, Abraham is no longer the center of the story. There is no need to call attention primarily to his actions. Indeed, we would expect the fact that Isaac accompanied Abraham to be noted in order to show that the unity of father and son was preserved and even enhanced. During the trial and tribulation, Abraham is shown to act fully in conformity as a partner of God.

Notes

1. Earlier the word *covenant* is mentioned to Abram during a dream (15:18): "On that day the Lord made a covenant with Abram saying, To your offspring I give this land . . . " The only other mention of covenants is to Noah (6:18; 9:9–11). However, these apply to general mankind and not to a particular people, as is the case with Abraham. Furthermore, the covenants with Noah do not consist of mutual continuous obligations, as was the case with Abraham (17:2).
2. These conflicts in Abraham's mind are imaginatively brought out in the Midrash on the Akedah. See L. Ginsberg, *The Legends of the Jews,* vol. 1 (Philadelphia: Jewish Publication Society, 1947), pp. 279–286.
3. Contradictions were also used as a device for man to acquire the "knowledge of good and evil." See part A, chapter III.

PART B

The Application of the Concepts Developed in Part A to Some Religious Aspects

God's challenge to man to accept the assignment of the responsibility for the morality of this world (part A) is ever-present in life. In assuming this responsibility, man is fully aware that in the choices he makes the presence of God is always present in the form of His challenge. The possibility of communication between God and man is discussed.

Chapter VI

Revelation: Resolving the Conflict in Communication between the Infinite and Finite Orders of Being

Revelation is the quintessential part of Jewish theology. Conditions of its occurrence must, therefore, be investigated. "In Jewish philosophy, the term 'revelation' embraces a variety of meanings, ranging from the supernatural communication of divine truth and instruction to the apprehension of God's will and attributes through the exercise of man's spiritual or rational faculties."[1] This explanation authorizes the concept of possible progressive or multitudinous revelations that are not mutually consistent and may even be contradictory. Historically, this has led to all kinds of divisions among people. It is to these divisions that religious persecution can be attributed. Modern man, however, questions or denies the actuality, or even the possibility, of supernatural revelation, once regarded as the only source of religious truth. In principle, it is contended, God cannot reveal anything of Himself to man. (Since God is unknowable, He cannot reveal anything about Himself; if He did, He would be knowable and thus would not be God.)

Emil L. Fackenheim claims that either revelation is the direct gift of God to man or it is not revelation at all.[2] But this is irrelevant, because God's incursion into time and temporality is not possible, for God, being infinite, cannot enter into the temporal. Communication between the infinite and finite mind is not possible, as indicated in a conclusion suggested by Maimonides, that communication can occur only among members of the same species.

Revelation at Sinai occurs, traditionally speaking, when God descends. However, His being in eternity, He cannot descend, at least in the sense of being transmuted into time, for if He did, He would cease to be God.[3]

Does this mean that man has to live without the benefit of revelation from God?

What, then, can we say about a God-man relationship that would circumvent the major objection of an infinite God making His knowledge or direction known to finite man? I suggest that there is such a possibility. This is *God's revelation in the process of creation*. If any revelation *to man* were possible, it would have had to occur in the process of creation, prior to his being doomed to die, i.e., prior to his becoming mortal. Once creation was finished completely, revelation would mean God's intervention in history.

According to Genesis 1, God created the physical world by divine fiat: "Let there be . . . " This applied to all creation *with the exception of man*. The creation of order out of chaos provided the basis for mathematical and physical laws according to which nature has to express itself. The movement in this physical world became limited; thus a stone falls downward, but it is not possible for it to fall upward. Physical events follow those laws of nature, fixed, impersonal principles that can be discovered through observation and reasoning and stated in mathematical terms. This represented the first revelation of the Divine Will. *Creation is, therefore, Revelation.*

When man was to be created, God did not use the same method of creation as He used for the creation of the world. "Let there be" gave way to "Let us make man in our image" (1:26) and was followed by the purpose of man's creation, while purpose was lacking in the creation of the animals. This was a significant change, which set man apart from all other creation and conferred upon him one facet of humanity. Not only did God make man in "His image," which is generally interpreted to mean possessing reason, intellect, imagination, free will, etc. (a knowing agent), but revealed man's purpose: to "rule the world and have dominion over it" (1:28). The purpose for which man was created required the "image" relationship or the knowledge of mathematics, physics, and the sciences. Without these, the delicately balanced order of the universe could not be understood and explicated by man to determine the nature within which man found himself. *This was also a revelation by God,* though of a different character from before.

The next revelation of the Divine Will *represented the creation of the moral and spiritual faculties of man.*[4] God took clay and molded man out of it and then breathed life into him. As a result of this action, man became a spiritual being. The moral aspect of man was, then, achieved by challenging Adam with a choice of whether to partake of the Tree of Knowledge of Good and Evil. As he was endowed with reason, the choice would be a result of his own autonomous analysis. Thus he would become aware of the condition of morality, the second aspect of humanity (a moral agent).

This third revelation was necessary as a counterpoise to man's exercise of the rulership and dominion over the physical world. It imposes restraints on man's tendency and desire to abuse nature for his selfish purposes. A more important aspect of this revelation was to establish man's relation to God and, therefore, man-to-man relationships. The three revelations, all universal, flow logically—the creation of the physical world, the creation of the man of reason and intellect to have dominion over the world, and, finally, the creation of moral man to become aware of the knowledge of good and evil through his autonomous choice as a consequence of his own analysis of the contradictions inherent in the choice posed by God. These three revelations are sufficient to mark man with the responsibility of existence (both in the physical and moral realms) and as a partner of God. No other revelations are necessary. Neither are they possible, because of the unbridgeable chasm between the infinite God and the finite mind, or between eternity and temporality.

The permanence of creation speaks of permanence of revelation inherent in it. This revelation has become the essence of this people's (Israel's) existence. God would ever challenge man and in so doing require anew a choice, a response and action by man as a partner of God and as one responsible for existence of this world, in both the physical and moral realms.

Revelation, as interpreted here, does not excuse Jews from the need to learn from practical experience, nor does it make unnecessary all knowledge gained through human effort. To the contrary, it makes it necessary. The Torah was offered to Israel by Moses, and the Israelites accepted it freely and autonomously, in accordance with their free will. There was no promise of reward if they accepted the Torah of Moses nor fear of punishment if their decision was to reject it. It was their newly found freedom that created the necessary condition for their action. Their decision to accept the Torah was, therefore, autonomous and represented Jewish identity in its most striking aspect—the acceptance of partnership with God.

One may question whether the event at Sinai was revelation. The Five Books (Pentateuch) are referred to as the Torah of Moses. He had just led the Israelites to freedom. A document was required to explain the history, the destiny, the instruction, and the community relationships to keep the group of former slaves united in a cohesive national unit. This is likely the reason for inclusion not only of moral laws of obvious social utility, but nonmoral laws, ritual laws for which no rational explanation can be found except that they were intended to maintain the separateness and holiness[5] of the nation. Also, man needs a system of observances to give concrete expression to his religious ideals and strivings. For forty days and nights Moses was alone, during which time he underwent a spiritual inspiration to compose the Torah (an I-Thou encounter resulting in Moses providing the language and content of the Torah and God His presence). When Moses came down with the Torah, the six hundred thousand Israelites became aware that the content of that document must have represented God's word. The people became committed to the Torah.

The crossing of the Red Sea and the plagues may be considered natural phenomena that could be claimed in the name of God, as God had made special provisions for these things during creation, because direct intervention of God in man's life is not possible.

The prophets were not expressing new revelation. In the name of God they often dealt with the challenges of the present. Their utterances are marked by penetrating insights into the socioeconomic and political realities of the ancient world, and their concerns were love, justice, and humility. While they spoke in the name of God (*Navi* means "spokesman"), they expressed their moral and spiritual perceptions in line with what they thought the Torah and covenant taught. They were interested in the Torah, in the laws the Israelites were expected to follow, but mainly in the moral and the covenantal responsibilities, not cultic practices.

Notes

1. *Encyclopedia Judaica*, 1st edition. vol. 14: *Modern Jewish Philosophy*, p. 124.
2. Emil L. Fackenhcim, *Quest for Past and Future* (Bloomington and London: Indiana University Press, 1968), p. 106.
3. Ibid., p. 67.
4. Part A, chapter 3.
5. Kadosh means "separate and holy."

Chapter VII
Covenant: Resolving the Disjunction of God and Man

The essential way of understanding the Jewish covenant is that it presupposes as well as establishes a fundamental relationship between God and Israel. As such, the covenant constitutes the very essence of the idea of Jewish religious phenomena. This is expressed in Paul Ramsey's formulation: "Never imagine that you have rightly grasped a biblical idea until you have reduced it to a corollary of the idea of 'covenant.' "[1] The point is that the religious view, as opposed to the philosophical view, lies not in apprehending God as He is in Himself, but in grasping the relationship that exists between God and man.[2]

The pagan cultures of the ancient Near East recognized many existing covenants between individuals and nations, e.g., suzerain-vassal treaties. The genius of ancient Israel lay precisely in its capacity to transform a horizontal relationship into a vertical one as well. This may not be surprising, since the Israelites considered God as their King.[3] The covenantal relationship as reflected in the Bible in the Sinaitic covenant seems to be patterned after the suzerain-vassal model. However, there are factors that make the Sinaitic covenant unique. There is respect for human freedom before God, since entry into the covenant is a matter of autonomous choice. Though Moses, in the name of God, took the initiative in offering the Torah to Israel, the Torah was not imposed on Israel by God, which is contrary to the suzerain-vassal treaty, in which the stronger power imposes on the weaker.

In the ancient Near Eastern suzerain-vassal treaty as we know it, the vassal does not ratify *verbally* the treaty, as Israel does at Sinai. Freedom is present in another sense. Israel is left with the freedom to develop and interpret the covenantal provisions. Dilbert R. Hillers states that the covenant idea plays a large part in giving Israel's religion its distincitive character in comparison to religions of her neighbors, almost as much as did her characteristic monotheism.[4] The distinctiveness of the covenant is seen in Exodus 19:5–6: "... if you keep the covenant ye shall be unto Me a Kingdom of priests and a holy nation."

The development of the covenant in the Bible is an interesting phenomenon. It starts with a unilateral promise and proceeds to the fully developed form in the Sinaitic covenant. The evolution of the covenant can be observed during the life of Abraham. The relationship with Abraham begins with promissory covenants[5] that Abraham's descendants will become a great nation, that his dependents will be as numerous as the dust and stars in the heavens, and that specific lands will belong to him.[6] The promissory covenant did not require any responsibility or actions by Abraham. Then, in Genesis 17:1–2, God introduces Himself as El Shaddai and requires that Abraham "walk in My ways and be blameless." No explanation is given as to how Abraham is to carry out these instructions or to their meaning.

In Genesis 17:5, God changes Abram's name to Abraham, which, in the ancient world, denoted a new destiny. Abraham would be the father of a multitude of nations. The covenant, the sign of which is circumcision, will represent an *everlasting* covenant throughout the ages. The land of Canaan will belong to Abraham, and the covenant will be maintained through Isaac. The word *everlasting* means that the covenant cannot be broken, either by God or man, but it may be suspended, as noted when the conditional element is introduced: "For I have singled him out, that he may instruct his children and his posterity to keep the way of the Lord by doing what is just and right in order that the Lord may bring about for Abraham what He has promised him" (18:19). Thus God will not keep His part of the promise unless man "does what is just and right." The promise by God is contingent upon man's prior actions. But then what happens to the eternity of the covenant?

In addition to the conditional element of the statement, a phrase is mentioned that deserves explanatory comments: The phrase "for I have singled him out" implies that God chose Abraham to establish a covenant with him. This state of chosenness has much greater implication than *chosen* or *singled him out*. The word *chosen* implies duty and obligations rather than privileges, as the complete citation above (18:19) denotes. In modern times, however, the interpretation of chosenness has been that the Jews chose God and, *therefore, God had to reciprocate and choose the Jews.*[7] While the modern interpretation seems to be inconsistent with the phrase "I have singled him out," it is my claim that the modern interpretation is more correct than the traditional view. My question is: why did God single out Abraham instead of someone else? The answer is relatively simple. Abraham was the first person to establish the concept of ethical monotheism as being wholly different from polytheistic concepts involving an agent above the human species and concerned with morality. "Shall not the Judge of all the earth deal justly?" (18:25) Abraham asks, seeking justification for his newly found concept. Thus the process of chosenness was initiated by a man who understood that the world has to recognize God as being moral for the benefit of humanity.

Returning to the subject under discussion, we find that there are additional covenants of promise that finally led to the central covenant in Judaism mediated by Moses at Sinai. Thus the history of the covenant begins with unconditional promissory acts (in which man is a silent, passive recipient), followed by a covenant requiring minimal participation by man to whom the requirement is not spelled out in a definitive statement (doing what is just and right).[8] It depends solely on man's autonomous, though not arbitrary, interpretation of their meanings. Finally, this process ends in a covenant specifying definite responsibilities and obligations on the part of man and, furthermore, emphasizes the conditional element inherent in the covenant, i.e.:

> But if you do not obey Me and do not observe all these commandments, if you reject My laws and spurn My rules, so that you do not observe all My commandments and you break My covenant, I in turn will do this to you: I will wreak misery upon you—consumption and fever, which cause the eyes to pine and the body to languish; you shall sow your seed to no purpose, for your enemies shall eat it. I will set My face against you: you shall be routed by your enemies, and your foes shall dominate you. You shall flee though none pursues. [Leviticus 26:14–17]

Throughout the Bible, many conditional elements are in evidence. All indicate that reward will follow if God's commandments are obeyed and punishment will result if the people do not follow them. The question is whether performance by man according to the commandments results in a situation that would call forth consequences that might necessarily follow.

Every covenant, including the one at Sinai, represents to some extent a divine self-limitation. If a law is given to Israel by God to be observed either in its positive or negative connotation, the law binds God as well. If God demands justice, then Abraham had the duty to question God. "Shall not the Judge of all the earth deal justly?" Abraham was justified in his action because God was patient with his repetitive questions.

A Modern Reinterpretation of the Covenant

As stated above, the covenant is a relational construct. The covenant at Sinai in Exodus calls for God to enter the temporal realm and to communicate with the finite mind of man. God, being infinite and eternal, cannot enter the sphere of temporal time and space, for this would preclude his being God.[9] What, then, happens to the covenant or the relationship between man and God? For that we have to go back to the time of creation and the story of Adam II, when man had not yet become finite and entered the temporal world. Man was created *in* the image[10] of God (man is not *the* image of God), which elevated him above the other creatures of the world. The "image" relationship, in itself, denotes a covenant and partnership. Adam, the archetype of man, having been created with reason, freedom, and intellect and having been assigned the dominion of the earth, thus becomes a partner of God. This represents a covenental relationship in the physical domain.

The narrative of Adam II deals with the moral and spiritual realm. Part A of this book deals with this narrative, in which it is shown that God's charge to Adam II to refrain from eating of the fruit of the Tree of Knowledge of Good and Evil was, in reality, a challenge for Adam II to determine the real meaning of the negative charge by resolving the contradictions that God's demand entailed. Adam II concluded that God actually wanted him to eat of the tree and thus obtain the knowledge of good and evil (the difference between them), good and evil belonging to the texture of nature. By this knowledge Adam became a potential moral being. In this manner, God assigned the responsibility of the moral realm to mankind, which Adam autonomously accepted, and thus a covenantal relationship with God was established.

The covenant having been established, Adam could enter an earthly existence, for which he was prepared when he was assigned the dominion of the physical world (1:28). As an act of free will, Adam accepted the responsibility of the moral realm, which leads one to approach all acts in a spirit of responsible freedom. Man thus becomes the partner of God, which, as stated previously, may be seen implicitly in the image relationship, the word *image* being understood as meaning "representative" of God.

In this manner, creation, revelation, and covenant are completely integrated and established prior to historical time and space. There is no necessity for traditional Judaism to maintain that revelations or covenants occur at specific times and places in the history of Israel, which violates the possibility of God, infinite and eternal, manifesting Himself in the temporal and finite or bridging the chasm between the finite mind and the infinite. Revelation would also violate the Maimonidean concept of the unknowability of God. The covenantal statements in the Bible should be understood as nothing more than incessant aspiring by man to scale the ladder of understanding God and spirituality in order to be able to exercise partnership with God and to make the responsible choices.

Creation involves an irreducible separation between the physical world and God. However, with the creation of the potential moral and spiritual man in a covenantal relationship with God, a divine challenge to man remains and persists in life, which is addressed to mankind. Man continuously faces choices in life, and the challenges present in life help man to resolve the choices with an autonomous moral responsibility. Judaism is the only religion recognizing this covenantal challenge throughout one's life.

Notes

1. Paul Ramsey, "Elements of a Biblical Theory," *Journal of Religion* no. 5 (1949): 258.
2. The narrative about the Adam test defines the relationship between God and man. See part A, in chapters 3 and 4, in which this idea is developed.
3. In ancient times, there were many instances, e.g., Egypt, in which the rulers were considered divine. The perception of their divinity, however,

was not the same as that of Israel, which viewed God as the Creator and not as a mortal being.
4. Dilbert R. Hillers, *Covenant: The History of the Biblical Idea* (Baltimore, MD: Johns Hopkins Press, 1969).
5. A promissory covenant is also stated after the Flood, in which God promises not to destroy the world again by flood (9:11).
6. Genesis 12:1–3; 12:7; 13:14–17; 15:1–5.
7. See part B, chapter 10.
8. No mention of cultic observances, but only moral actions (doing what is just and right).
9. Emil L. Fackenheim, *Quest for Past and Future* (Bloomington and London: Indiana University Press, 1968), p. 67.
10. Saadya (888–982 C.E.) already associated the image of God in Genesis with humanity's Godlike rule over creation.

Chapter VIII
Prayer: Addressing the Other in the Partnership of God and Man

The concept of prayer is based on the conviction that God exists, that He is a personal deity and thus hears and answers as His will dictates. That God hears prayers is shown by Psalm 65:3:

O Thou that hearest prayer,
Unto Thee doth all flesh come.

Prayer is essentially emotional in character even though it displays an intellectual base. It is an expression of man's attempt to unburden his soul before God and man's quest for the Divine.

Like a hind crying for water,
My soul cries for You, O God;
My soul thirsts for God, the living God;
O when will I come to appear before God?

—Psalm 42:2–3

or:

Trust in Him, at all times, O People;
Pour out your hearts before Him;
God is our refuge.

—Psalm 62:9

The rabbis called prayer "the service of the heart." However, the needs of man being numerous and complex, prayer inescapably came to reflect the vast range of human needs, praise, hopes, fears, feelings, and aspirations. In the patriarchal period, a simple invocation of God's name was sufficient. God, at that time, was near, marked by directness and familiarity. Later on, God was addressed directly for a sign or oracle or indirectly through a priest or a prophet. However, in an emergency, man sought help in the future by entreating God's help. Thus Abraham sought salvation for Sodom (18:23–33), Joshua sought divine help in the hour of defeat (Joshua 7:6–9), and the prophets beseeched God on behalf of their people (Jeremiah 14:1; Amos 7:2). Solomon's dedicatory prayer at the consecration of the Temple (I Kings 8:12–53) includes almost every type of prayer—adoration, thanksgiving, petition, and confession. The range of biblical prayer thus extends from the simplest needs to the highest spiritual yearnings.

Sacrifice and prayer persisted until the destruction of the Second Temple. The combination of the two can be traced back to the Patriarchs:

> . . . the site of the altar which he had built there at first; and there Abram invoked the Lord by name.
> —Genesis 13:4

or:

> So he built an altar there, and invoked the Lord by name. Isaac pitched his tent there and his servants started to dig a well.
> —Genesis 26:25

In the synagogue, prayer, together with Scripture readings and exposition, took the place of altar offerings. There are many different types of prayers—prayers of intercession; confessional and penitential prayers; worship and adoration prayers; trust-in-God prayers; requests-for-divine-help-and-deliverance prayers; requests-for-mercy prayers; thanksgiving and requests-for-healing prayers; and many others. All are directly addressed to God; nearly all call for action by God.

In the model of theology set forth in this work, what is the function of prayer? Assuming that man was assigned the responsibility for this world, argued above, and that he freely commits himself to this responsibility, prayer would no longer be an appeal for help from God. Rather, prayer would be the act by means of which man tries to reach beyond his own being. Through prayer, man admires the majesty of creation and senses the wonder of the divine image in his heart.

> Yet Thou hast made him but little lower than angels, and Thou hast crowned him with glory and honor. Thou hast made him to have dominion over the works of Thy hand . . .
> —Psalm 8:6, 7

Through prayer, man contemplates his relationship with God and his own human responsibilities. Man realizes that his soul is closer to God than to the universe with its innumerable galaxies. The worshiper feels that his efforts to deal with the problems and concerns of the world form part of the movement of the world toward the perfection of earthly existence. As a partner of God, man not only sees his human needs, especially in the light of his overriding concern for self-fulfillment; he understands, moreover and more importantly, his purpose and the will of God, which is established through God-man partnership.

In prayer, man addresses the Other. However, being a partner, man's will is synonymous with the will of the Other. Thus in prayer man addresses himself.

Prayer is also Torah study by which man shows that he belongs to the congregation of Israel, i.e., the community of partners of God. Study is a form of prayer just as prayer is a form of study. The two are interlinked. Perhaps the most characteristic quality of the Jewish prayer is its emphasis on Torah learning. Torah, understood in this way, assumes an additional meaning, that of rational self-reflection and self-criticism.

Jews pray as partners of God—for God's Will to be done through us. Thus, we are responsible for acting out the Divine Will as partners of God who understand His challenge to mankind.

The issue of prayer is not prayer per se; the issue is man's attempt to increase his understanding of spirituality and morality. Prayer is not for the sake of acquisition, but to be with someone; it is to be open to an I-Thou encounter. Prayer is the way God enters our life in terms of man's relation to Him.

The Jew directs his attention to the God of Abraham, Isaac, and Jacob, with whom he identifies himself as a partner, not the God of the philosophers, not the God of truth, beauty, and goodness. The Jewish view today establishes the God of Abraham, Isaac, and Jacob but does not exclude understanding God in other, broader terms.

Prayer expresses hope. It acknowledges the presence of the challenge of God. In prayer, one is immersed in the thought that man is created in the image of God and that God's image is in his soul, attaining its fullest potential only through his own efforts. In prayer, one does not think about the self; rather, one is directed toward the realization that God and man are partners in the process for the final redemption of the world. One contemplates the charge by God to man that man is essentially the prime force in this process and is God's instrument through which His will is carried out. Prayer articulates man's ideals, makes him conscious of the goals that he professes internally, and strengthens his determination to attain them.

Prayer lifts us out of our immediate situations, establishes a bond with our fellow Jews, fellowman, and previous generations. It makes us think about human life as a whole and about our existence in particular; it makes us more aware and thoughtful about the social and ethical problems of our days. In prayer, we are ever mindful of the statement of Cain: "Sin lies at the door, but you can master it" (4:7).

Chapter IX
Forgiveness: What Can Be Forgiven and Who Can Forgive

Repentance is a prerequisite for forgiveness. Repentance requires genuine remorse for the wrong one has committed and then the conversion of this penitential commitment into concrete acts of morality. This commitment, however, cannot be fulfilled by a dying man. In a sense, then, the repentance of such a man is imperfect. This deficiency is particularly evident where absolution is sought for the transgression of murder. In such a case, forgiveness cannot be granted except by God.

In the Bible, all expressions of men's penitential acts are summarized by one word, שוב (to return) which develops ultimately into the rabbinic concept of *teshuvah*, repentance. The word combines both requisites for repentance: to turn from evil and to do good. (The Christian concept of repentance is different and will be discussed later on in this chapter.) In my view, it means the abandonment of one position (choice to do evil) and the adoption of the opposite position (choice to do good). It does not permit the choice of indifference.

The primary requirement for forgiveness involves the heart and conscience of man. Inner contrition must be translated into deeds.

The term *return* (שוב) means that a person who had strayed from a positive position has returned to that positive position. An example of this is Rosenzweig, who had turned from Judaism to Western culture, even to the point of considering becoming a Christian, and then returned to Judaism. Rosenzweig speaks to the hyphenated Jew, i.e., one who has been strongly influenced by non-Jewish cultural values. In the thought of Martin Buber, the idea of repentance is essentially the turning of the whole man to God, the Eternal Thou. In Buber, in turning to God no positive action to do good is required. The turning itself, in which the Thou is encountered, represents the positive good.

Forgiveness depends on the type of crime, the degree of evil, and the reason the crime was committed. Forgiveness also depends on the religion and culture of the individual who has committed the crime for which he seeks forgiveness. Certain categories of sinners should never be forgiven by men because of the nature of the crimes. Among such crimes are desecration of God's name, to be forgiven only by God, and murder, which eliminates the presence of the only one who can provide forgiveness. For the purpose of this chapter we can dismiss crimes that do not involve murder. I am interested only in murder and genocide. I do not imply that the other crimes are insigificant and do not result in pain and suffering or in the degradation of the victim. Such cases are easier to act upon because they do not involve ultimate concerns. This problem is illustrated by Simon Wiesenthal[1]: Can a Jew forgive a Nazi stormtrooper when he confesses to the crimes he committed and asks for forgiveness? Is it moral not to forgive when the Nazi repents on his death bed? How would this problem be answered in my *The Challenge of God to Man: A Theology of Responsible Freedom*?

Before we answer these questions, we must examine the nature of the crime that was the Holocaust and its relation to both Jewish and Christian thought and theologies. The horror that was the Holocaust is beyond human imagination and brings language to the breaking point. Can we imagine the deaths of 6 million human beings and their unborn children simply because they were born into the Jewish faith by chance? They were not Jewish by choice, yet they were murdered in cold blood, in a deliberate, systematic, efficient manner in the center of Christianity by Christians, a Christianity that claims as their Savior a Jew, a son of the Jewish God who lived as a Jew and died as a Jew and therefore was resurrected as a Jew.

The Holocaust is a unique event in history. It transcends all tragic events; it is an epoch-making event. It is so because human history and metaphysics cannot be the same since the Holocaust. After the Holocaust, any thinking about human nature and God must be done with the death camps, burning children, and the memory of the innocent victims in mind. It was a period of ultimate evil that surpassed the evil of Hiroshima, Bangladesh, Afghanistan, and other places. The genocide of the Jewish people was an end in itself—regardless of the ways in which political and economic factors may initially have contributed to the stigmatization of the Jews in German eyes. The theological root of this stigma had its basis in Christian Scriptures and its elaboration in both the Catholic and Protestant traditions. Luther himself was one of its principal expositors. It was the attempt at the total reconstruction of the world to Ultimate Evil. There was no evidence of responsibility by the Germans except to Hitler, who personified ultimate evil. This evil involved all acts against morality and life in the name of death. The Jew was singled out for murder for being essentially who he was, as well as what he was. If the Jews had all been killed in the Final Solution, then the Jewish love of freedom, the profound love of life as lived on earth as each responsible individual sees it, the insistence that there is no separation between the divine and the human acts, a sense of human responsibility to and for each other, the refusal of blind obedience to the authoritarian state would have diminished to a minimum.

Nazism could not tolerate such principles. Thus the murder of all Jews was expressed in the formula of the Final Solution.

This term is very informative. It implies other attempts at eliminating the Jews, and it recalls Haman, the Inquisition, the Crusades, and the pogroms in Russia and Poland, as well as the wholesale removal of the Jews from the lands of their birth. (There were about three hundred such removals in European history.) Indeed, Hitler told two Catholic bishops that he was just doing to the Jews what the Catholic church had been trying to do to them for nearly two thousand years. More than one Nazi war criminal referred to Luther as justification for their actions. Luther's language was very similar to the language used by Nazis. (Luther's statements about the Jews are shown in another part of this chapter.)

Although, on one level, the Holocaust represents a metaphysical problem, its most immediate impact is felt in the domain of the historical, where irresponsibility and indifference stood as the accomplice to the willful perpetration of evil. Therefore, it remains repeatable. There is no break in the line from the charge of deicide and punishment to Hitler's death camps, and the line is still unbroken by lack of repentance on the part of the Church.

In this case, forgiveness is not even a question to be discussed. The Christian Church, having been silent during the Holocaust, expressed complicity with ultimate evil. In this respect, the Church remained faithful to the New Testament's condemnation of Jews who refused to accept the messianic claims of Jesus. In the language of some Christian theologians—only too few—the New Testament is wrong in the claim that Jews killed Jesus. It is also wrong in advocating that Christianity has replaced Judaism in God's plan and that Jews must convert to Christianity in order to be saved. Is it any wonder that the Christians were imbued with anti-Semitism, which provided fertile soil for Nazi indoctrination that Jews were the children of the Devil and, therefore, must be murdered?

Cynthia Ozick states in *The Sunflower*: "Forgiveness does not condone or excuse. It allows for redemption and permits renewal. But only if there is a next time. With murder there is no 'next time.' Will the murdered come alive again? We forgive when there is a next time, as when children misbehave." Ozick says further: "Forgiveness is pitiless. It forgets the victim. It negates the right of the victim to his own life. It blurs over suffering and death. It drowns the past. It cultivates sensitiveness toward the murderer at the price of insensitiveness toward the victim."[2]

While the Nazi hell continued, forgiveness at that time became complicity. When this hell stopped, one could be thankful, but to forgive the conceivers or the murderers of the Holocaust is not incumbent upon our consciences. Neither is vengeance, for that would only pile evil upon evil. What remains in importance is only memory. It is this that acts as a shield for reoccurrence; it says, "Never again."

The German of intelligence and culture of this period must be condemned because he allowed himself to be dehumanized. If he had a conscience, he allowed himself to become a savage. That German is worse than the one who was a savage to begin with. Such a person can never be forgiven for this betrayal of humanity.

Forgiveness for a crime is within the province of the victim only. No one else can forgive. In case of murder, there is no one who can forgive. Can a Jew, as a representative of the Jewish victims, forgive an SS man? Can a Jew forgive an SS man, who represents a genocidal community? Forgiving an SS man would by implication forgive all SS men who murdered. Genocide is a collective concept. This can never be forgiven, because forgiveness is but the first stage of forgetting. We cannot come to terms with this event. While genocide is collective, the crimes of murder were committed by individuals who vied with others in the degree and horror of their violence. The rapidity of the extermination of the Jews speaks of the state of mind of the SS man. He relished the crimes he committed. As many Germans had been raised in the tradition of Martin Luther, a genocidal concept was a logical consequence. Listen to the words of Luther:

> Jews want to rule the world and already dominate many good Christians; they are arch-criminals, killers of Christ and Christendom; they are a plague, pestilence and pure misfortune.

Among his remedies:

> . . . burning synagogues, burning Jewish homes, since in these Judaism is practiced; confiscating religious books; prohibiting rabbis the teaching of Judaism on the pain of death; prohibiting Jewish travel; prohibiting Jewish moneylending and confiscating gold and silver.

Martin Luther thought that Jews would accept his beliefs. When the Jews resisted his views, Luther adopted a most hateful policy toward them, as shown above. What a short step from this attitude to genocide!

It may have happened that a storm trooper, observing the evil being perpetrated in the camps, experienced pangs of conscience and decided to discontinue such acts and ask for forgiveness. His repentance might be sincere, in which case it would have to be demonstrated by active opposition to the Nazis, not merely abstaining from committing the crimes. He would have to save Jews to repent for the Jews he had killed. In such a case, forgiveness might be in order. But what of the SS man asking forgiveness on his deathbed? He could not be forgiven because his sincerity is open to question and he could not do any penance. Perhaps he was motivated to ask for forgiveness to save his soul and not for any change of conscience. The young Nazi in *The Sunflower* could have asked a priest for forgiveness, but he felt that forgiveness by a Jew would be more efficacious. A Nazi on his deathbed who is a Catholic can be forgiven only by a priest;

no Jew can forgive him. For a Jew to forgive him would be tantamount to killing the victim twice.

Murder and genocide are different in the sense that murder is committed against individuals for profit or vengeance, while genocide has ultimate evil as its purpose; the murder of a whole community for profit is not its driving force. It is sheer murder for the sake of murder. It simply makes statements such as: "As a Jew, you have no right to life." Therefore, a Jew cannot engage in any thought of forgiveness. In remembering the act we must also remember the perpetrator. Since the act and the perpetrator are intimately connected, forgiveness is not to be, especially since in forgiveness we neglect the victim.

In genocide, the perpetrators are faceless. In that case, the whole generation is responsible. This includes the Church officials, philosophers, writers, Ph.D.'s intelligentsia, etc., who allowed their consciences to be dulled and allowed the process of brutalization to proceed by indifference and finally entering the world of evil by dropping any pretense of conscience. Not only had this generation been indoctrinated into the evil, but their children's generation had also been infected. The seeds of evil will remain for several generations, as the resurgence of neo-Nazism demonstrates. Biblically, the concept of God not forgiving the evil acts of the fathers for several generations supports this statement.

Louise Rinser (a well-known German author and specialist in psychology) cites Jesus' statement about forgiveness: "... for they know not what they do."[3] The Nazis knew only too well what they were doing. This quotation is, therefore, not applicable. Furthermore, whom did Jesus have in mind when he uttered these words? Not the Jews who did not participate in the Crucifixion; not the Romans, who could not possibly know and understand the "divinity" of Jesus but were troubled by a "King of the Jews." Perhaps he meant his disciples, who had faith in him but deserted him because they feared for their own lives.

They did not understand the redemptive act of God taking place. Rinser does not mention the cry of Jesus on the cross, "God, God, why have you forsaken me?" (Psalms 22). Indeed, this is hardly heard of anymore. Is it possible that Jesus felt abandoned by God and did not know that God's redemptive event was taking place? Otherwise, why charge God with forsaking him if, as a son of God, he would have thanked God for the redemptive act taking place for which he was sent into the world?

To illustrate the complexity of forgiveness, I will quote Jacques Maritain (a well-known French philosopher and professor at Princeton and Columbia Universities) who suggests that Wiesenthal should have said: "I could forgive you only for any wrong you have done to me personally. How, though, could I, in their names, forgive you for the atrocities you committed against others? What you have done is, humanely speaking, unforgivable. But, *in the name of your God, yes, I forgive you.*" (Italics are Maritain's.)[4] This represents nothing more than imposing the Christian concept of forgiveness upon the Jew. Then, I may ask, why has Christianity never forgiven the Jews for deicide over the past two thousand years, even though they were not guilty? It is also interesting to note that the dying SS man in *The Sunflower* was never forgiven by his own Christian father for joining the Nazi party. It is poetic justice that he died without forgiveness by his father and by Wiesenthal; neither one spoke to him.

How does this incident fare in my proposed theology? According to my theology, man is responsible for the morality of this world. God charged him with this responsibility. In accepting the charge, man is also assigned to be the judge of man's actions. A man's crimes can take many forms. They may range from a poor man's stealing bread to feed his children to the ultimate, monstrous crime of the Holocaust—the murder of a whole people from causeless hatred.

Forgiveness, then, also falls within man's province, with the exception of verbal acts defaming God or building idols as the object of prayer in the mistaken notion that the idol controls the fortunes of man. This can be forgiven only by God. Courts deal with legal matters. In matters of morality, courts have no jurisdiction. Only man, who is committed to the responsibility of existence (being a partner of God), may judge on the question of morality. Having said this, I reiterate: the only one who can forgive is one who suffered harm by the action of another.

But are there crimes that can never be forgiven by man, who is committed to the responsibility for the morality of existence? Man cannot forgive murder or the crimes of the Holocaust. Both involve loss of life, which was given to us by God. Only God may forgive in such cases. Other crimes—degradation of humanity, such as rape or abuse of one's children, acts committed under the influence of alcohol or other drugs that affect the mind, or denying the civil rights of a person—may be forgiven provided repentance is sincere and proper restitution (*teshuvah*) is carried out. If man makes an error in forgiveness, God can deal with it later.

Notes

1. Simon Wiesenthal, *The Sunflower* (New York: Schocken Books, 1969).
2. Quoted in Wiesenthal, *The Sunflower,* pp. 185–86.
3. Ibid., p. 198.
4. Ibid., p. 171.

Chapter X
The Question of the Chosen People: The Agent of Choice

Much has been written on the question of Israel being the "Chosen People" of God. The interpretations range from the traditional concept, that God chose Israel by giving them the Torah in self-revelation at Sinai and thereby conferred upon the Jewish people the special distinction of His enduring providence, to such modern interpretations as those of Mordecai M. Kaplan, in which all claims of transcendental distinction are qualified, if not outrightly rejected.[1] Kaplan's interpretation is, as it were, suspended in midair, disconnected not only from the history of Jewish theology, but from Jewish history itself, i.e., from the past existence of the Jews, to whom the claim of being chosen provided the will and the power to continue their lives in spite of adversity, all the while feeling ennobled by the spiritual concept implied in their status of election and the belief of the prophetic vision of the messianic time to arrive.

Kaplan's view, of course, derives from his strong attachment to American democracy. He could not allow a view of chosenness to be superimposed on a portion of democratic people. Instead of questioning the *imposition* of the chosenness view, however, Kaplan destroyed the view of chosenness itself as well as the resultant relationship between God and the Jewish people. The alternative to Kaplan's position, however, does not require a return to traditional theologies of transcendence. It is possible, indeed necessary, to mediate the extremes. The following is a new interpretation that remains Jewish and keeps God and the Jews in their unique relationship. Essentially, it claims that it is man who originates the choosing and displays characteristics that make him qualified to be "chosen" by God.

The "chosenness" idea does not involve a "holier than thou" attitude, nor does it result in a sense of superiority on the part of the Jews. It neither mandates the belief that God favors the Jews to the exclusion of others nor justifies the expectation of future material rewards or special privileges. Indeed, it argues against all forms of parochialism to a genuinely universalist end.

The test of Adam II was to determine whether Adam II would opt for "the knowledge of good and evil." Adam II did choose this knowledge and, by this action, became "as God" (3:22). In this process, man became a potential partner of God in the moral and spiritual sphere. The active choice for man to become an actual partner lies in man's choice of good and in becoming committed to its fulfillment. Inasmuch as Adam I and Adam II may be considered as two different aspects of man, one of physical desires and one of morality, and since man is a descendant of Adam, all human beings are to be considered as partners of God, provided they choose the "knowledge of good and evil" and become committed to it. Thus the partnership concept represents a universal outlook.

In accordance with the preceding discussion that God's intention for mankind was to be His partners in the world, how then could Israel regard itself as the Chosen People or partners of God? The question bears examination. It is suggested that the universal appeal to man did not achieve God's intent. Therefore, since God's desire for mankind to opt for the partnership did not materialize, the procedure was adopted to work through individuals, a process that would finalize itself in a community with the mission of partnership, which would become its raison d'être.

In a definite sense, a person or a people is not chosen by God by grace, but in response to the requisites portrayed by them that reflect their choice of God in their moral and spiritual advances. The process of choosing or responding to the challenge of God starts with man. Once man chooses God, which is a basic choice, he enters into a relationship with God in which man accepts the responsibility of commitment to act as a partner of God, to act as he perceived God would want him to act. In this dynamic, man's choice and action represent the intent of God's Will and man's will is to fulfill God's Will. From man's view, the two wills become synonymous. Similarly, the Jewish people, through the process of evolutionary development of their precepts freely arrived at, and willing to demonstrate the moral and spiritual values, fulfilled the prerequisites required by God for a mission and example to the world.

Thus there are major factors that must be considered in this process of choice: the purpose and goal of the choice to be achieved and the appropriateness of the choice, or adequation of means and ends, i.e., the prerequisites required to be "chosen."

The prerequisites required in a choice must satisfy the purpose of the choice. A small wooden hammer will not be selected to demolish a ten-inch-thick steel wall. Similarly, for a specific person to be chosen by God, the person has to be able to carry out the intent of God and be a "choosing" person. A "choosing" person is one who, in facing problems, takes into account the knowledge of good and evil and is committed to the solution of the problem morally—thus responding to the challenge of God.[2]

The progression of prerequisites begins with Adam, who chose God's universalistic challenge of the "knowledge of good and evil," without which man cannot make a choice in the moral and spiritual sphere. Then came Noah, who is simply described as being righteous in his generation. The next person (Abraham) conceived of monotheism and expressed verbal commitment to morality by challenging God on the question of justice and rejected child sacrifice. Moses expressed full active commitment to moral problems by saving a slave, a Jew, even to the point of killing the overseer and thus showing responsibility to his people, Israel.

Israel, on being offered the Torah, accepted it as a guide for moral, spiritual, and legal behavior. The community of Israel is thus chosen by God. In the final step in the process of development of Jewish values are the prophets, whose views and visions reflected social justice, moral values, and spiritual relationship to God, which is the basis of their election by God to be prophets and true partners of God on the scale of the evolution of Jewish basic values.

God's challenge to the choosing person is for the benefit of that person. God knows what the person can do. This world was created to serve as the medium for human free-willed performance. When God challenges the choosing man, it is in order to permit him to translate potential into reality, as Psalm 115:16 states:

The Heavens belong to the Heavens above
The earth was given to the children of men

In light of the above, it is instructive to compare the order of progression of prerequisites the chosen people exhibited.

1. *Adam*. Genesis, to a large extent, deals archetypically with man—e.g., Adam and the tree, Cain–Abel, etc. These narratives are intended to reveal something *essential* for our understanding of man, something of the essence of the human situation and something that contributes to the relationship between man and God. This first act of choosing archetypically reveals a *positive* dimension of man and his immediacy in his relationship with God. Furthermore, subsequent biblical narratives in

Genesis can be understood as a *progression of this dimension*. Thus the Adam narrative expresses an original choice that enables man to *rise* in partnership with God by a deeper and more sensitive understanding of such values as justice, morality, compassion for his fellowman, goodness, etc. The first choice in history made by Adam presented the objective mankind faces—to establish a partnership relationship with God and to obtain the "knowledge of good and evil" that is necessary and fundamental to making other choices involving moral and spiritual attitudes.

2. *Noah*. The narrative of Noah present another archetypical situation. The world in his generation was corrupt, and the violence of man filled the earth (6:12–13). God in reaction to this situation decided to condemn the world. Noah's righteousness resulted in his being chosen to continue life. Noah walked with God (6:9), by which can be understood that he relied on the judgment of God and consequently did not question God on the issue of justice and mercy. This revealed that Noah lacked the element of responsibility for others. His was only a small step in the evolution of the partnership concept, because he still lived in a polytheistic culture. The comparison with Abraham is significant.

3. *Abraham*. Living in a polytheistic culture for many years, Abraham conceived of monotheism, which calls for the existence of only one God from whom all aspects of life derive. By this action Abraham changed the future of mankind. When God decided to destroy only two cities, Sodom and Gomorrah, unlike the case with Noah, which involved the whole world, Abraham's reaction was different and represented several degrees upward on the ladder of relationship and partnership with God above that of Noah. Abraham chose to question God on the issue of justice, and by his insistence Abraham demonstrated the right of man to question God on the issue of justice and morality. However, Abraham, by stopping at

ten people, failed to carry his responsibility to its final conclusion, by not arguing on behalf of innocent children and the unborn. Abraham also showed a lack of compassion in the case of Hagar and Ishmael. However, Abraham nevertheless was qualified to be chosen as a partner of God at this step of evolution of Judaism. Abraham in his choosing monotheism, in the resolution of the Akedah,[3] and in his sense of justice provided the necessary prerequisites to be chosen by God, as demonstrated by the establishment of the covenant.

4. *Moses*. He acknowledged the difference between good and evil, which led him to become involved with his people. His persuasive attitude to become actively committed and responsible for his fellow Jews qualified him to be chosen to lead the Jews to nationhood and to give them the cohesiveness by offering them the Torah.

5. *The Nation of Israel*. When Moses offered the Torah, which contained in it the spiritual, moral, and legal codes by which man could live, the answer was: "All that the Lord has spoken we will do" (Exodus 19:8). This indicated a prior commitment to the values to which their illustrious chosen predecessors already were committed. This stand of the Jews was a measure of their nature enabling them to be chosen. Israel represented a community setting in which the universalistic imprint of morality and spirituality was evident and had become part of the national psyche of the nation. Active commitment to morality was never abandoned. In Judaism, the human act of choosing God represents a self-imposed commitment to discharge the responsibilities of morality.

6. *The prophets*. A prophet is a unique person, not simply a mouthpiece; not an instrument, but a partner, an associate of God—a true partner who feels God's assignment of this world to man and, in spite of it, does not forsake God. The prophet has the ability to hold God and man in a single thought. He is a penetrating observer of the social contemporary scene.

His concern is with widows and orphans, the poor and the needy, corruption and affairs of the marketplace, and he is indignant about matters of injustice. To us, injustice is injurious to the welfare of the people; to the prophet, it is a deathblow to existence. The prophet is preoccupied with society and its conduct, not the issues of thought. Nothing that has a bearing upon good and evil is small and trite in the eyes of God, the prophet declares. The prophet is intent on intensifying human responsibility. Since the prophet acts as a partner of God and is committed to that relationship, his election by God is assured. To the prophet, God's presence is a challenge, an incessant demand for man to participate in partnership. It is noteworthy to point out that while man has the option of choosing or rejecting God, God has no such option but to choose man, because the intention of God is then fulfilled. God cannot choose a man who rejects him.

In sum, there are two parallel, though not concurrent, processes in the development of the idea of chosenness:

1. Man's progression as a choosing person necessary to be chosen by God for increasingly responsible tasks.
2. Man's progressive enhancement of the values in Judaism, which are seen as the direct consequence of man's prior development as a partner of God.

In this sense, Judaism is an evolving development of man's moral and spiritual values deriving from his continual responses to the challenges from God.

Notes

1. Mordecai M. Kaplan, *Judaism as a Civilization* (New York: McMillan, 1967). Kaplan claimed that the Jewish people "live with a sense of vocation

or calling, without involving ourselves in any invidious distinctions implied in the doctrine of the election, and yet to fulfill the legitimate spiritual wants which that doctrine sought to satisfy."
2. *Artscroll Tanach Series,* vol. 2: *On Genesis.* (Brooklyn, N.Y.: Mesorah Publications, 1978), p. 387. Rambam 22:1 states: "God will not test [choose] the wicked who will not obey."
3. See Part A, Chapter V.

Chapter XI

The Jewish and Christian Covenants and the Holocaust: The Role of Covenantal Thinking and the Origin of Auschwitz

For the purposes of this chapter, the complete details and manifestations of the Jewish and Christian covenants are not required and, therefore, will not be discussed. The discussion will restrict itself only to such features that illuminate the difference in the relations of the Christian covenant vis-à-vis the Jewish covenant. Without that difference, the Holocaust could not have occurred: that difference was the necessary, but not sufficient, reason for genocide.

What is the essential way of understanding the Jewish covenant? In the traditional view, it is chosenness, which establishes a fundamental relationship between God and Israel. The relationship, however, has much greater implications than the word *chosen*. Rather than conferring special privileges, the term *chosen* imposes extra obligations and responsibilities. This term is also subject to three differing interpretations:

1. God chose the Jews by Grace.
2. God chose the Jews because of their merit.
3. It was the Jews who chose God (and, therefore, God had to choose them). This interpretation is not transferable to Christianity.

The idea of chosenness by Grace was given classical articulation by the prophets, who also maintained that it implied duty rather than privilege e.g., Amos 3:2. On the other hand, Judah Halevi favors the merit principle. He claims that the Jewish people were endowed with a special religious faculty, first given to Adam and then bequeathed through a line of chosen representatives to all of Israel.[1]

The formulation of a third, new approach to the Jewish covenant has become necessary since the Holocaust in order to overcome the problems arising out of the current and traditional understanding of the covenantal relationship between God and the Jewish people. It is suggested that the divine-human covenant covers two different spheres of contribution and responsibility, each characteristic of the specific partner. In this view, God as the Creator endowed all human beings with free will and freedom of choice and also challenged man to accept the responsibility of existence, with particular emphasis on responsibility for the moral condition of the world, which represents God's contribution to the covenant. The human task, then, is to complete the covenant by accepting God's challenge. This acceptance translates into responsibility to become moral agents and, indeed, partners of God. The Torah, in expressing the sacredness of duty, provides the inescapable moral obligation and by its laws acts as a guide to moral perfection and teaches the discipline that helps prevent immoral and evil acts. The Torah is keenly aware of the problems of ethics.

The covenant is a relational category. In the context of the Jewish tradition, the covenant delineates the relations between man and God and between man and man. As such, it constitutes the very essence of religious phenomena; in Paul Ramsey's formulation, "Never imagine that you have rightly grasped a Biblical idea until you have reduced it to a corollary of the idea of 'covenant.' "[2] The point is that the religious view, as opposed to the philosophical view, lies not in apprehending God as He is in Himself, but in grasping the relation that exists between God and man.

The third conception of the Jewish covenant may be represented by a grid of vertical and horizontal components:

God

God's challenge to man to accept the responsibility for the moral condition of this world and become a partner of God.	Faith*

Action and Faith
The Social Element of Life.

Man   Man

This diagram expresses God's involvement in the totality of the life of the individual (not merely his "spiritual" side), His

---

*It is of interest to note the statement of James 2:19: "Faith without action is dead."

involvement in the community (the "political") aspect of life, and the *necessity for human cooperation for the fulfillment of the divine purpose in history*. Thus man needs God, as God needs man. One serves God by serving his fellowmen.

The horizontal level of relationship is the path through which Judaism is fulfilled on the vertical level. The purpose of the covenant is to establish a better world, a just and moral society that is strongly enunciated in the writings of the prophets and finds expression in rabbinic literature as well. Without the emphasis on the horizontal level of man-man relationship, the vertical component between God and man is greatly diminished. (This is observed in the precept that when man acts unjustly toward another man, he must first obtain forgiveness from the injured party before God will forgive him.) In the words of Isaiah 58:6–7:

> Loosen the chain of wickedness, and the bonds of oppression. Let the crushed go free, break all yokes of tyranny! Share your food with the hungry, take the poor to your home, Clothe the naked when you see them, never turn from your fellows.

That is, work to establish a more just and moral society. Thus it is up to man to make the covenant work and to realize the dream of eventual redemption. The statement from Psalms 115:16: "The Heavens belong to God, but the earth was given to the children of man," conforms well to this concept of covenant and confirms it. The Jewish acceptance of the responsibility of existence, in its broadest sense, means what Judaism figuratively calls *ol Malchut Shamayim* (the yoke of the Kingdom of Heaven), a responsibility that is freely chosen by the Jewish people. The Jewish image of the Jew is thus embodied in what is called a value stance, a specific cosmic attitude toward life and the world. This flows from the acceptance of the challenge of God, which gives birth to the *responsible* element of freedom. Without this, man is free to master others; with this, man is free to master only himself.

While Christians may see in Judaism an ethnic component to the exclusion of everybody else, universalism and ethnicity are not necessarily mutually exclusive. The totality of all ethnic groups composes universality. Indeed, this universalistic realization is exactly what Judaism envisions for the messianic era. The principle that the righteous of all nations have a share in the world to come similarly argues that the Jewish ethos constitutes a universal concept. The divine challenge to man to accept the responsibility for the moral condition of this world, first presented to Adam, is available to every person. Thus the covenant in Judaism always carried universal implications. Indeed, since no other religious outlook sees itself as a partner of God through the acceptance of the divinely assigned responsibility for this world, the Jews become a unique people.

What is the Christian view of the Christian covenant? Since Christianity grounds itself in Jewish Scriptures, its covenant also represents the fundamental category in its theological discourse. However, since Christianity understands the covenant differently, it represents on its fundamental level the points of difference between Judaism and Christianity. The essence of Christianity's covenant is soteriological, the doctrine of salvation through its Savior.

Before we proceed any further, it is necessary to point out that Christianity is not the religion of Jesus but is the religion about Jesus. The historical aspect of Jesus' life traditionally has occupied very little importance in Christianity, which puts its emphasis on the meaning of the death of Jesus and his resurrection, mainly found in Paul's teachings. Christianity at the same time refers to the teachings of Jesus, which were essentially Jewish. Several examples from St. Matthew may be cited:

> Do not think that I have come to do away with the Law of Moses and the teachings of the prophets. I have not come to do away with them, but to make their teachings come true.
> —Matthew 5:17

> Remember that as long as heaven and earth last, not the least point, not the smallest detail of the Law will be done away with—not until the end of all things.
> —Matthew 5:18

> If you are about to offer your gift at the altar and there you remember that your brother has something against you, leave your gift there in front of the altar, go at once and make peace with your brother, and come back and offer your gift to God.
> —Matthew 5:23

> Do for others what you want them to do for you: this is the meaning of the Law of Moses and of the teachings of the Prophets.
> —Matthew 7:12

There are several major aspects of the Christian covenant that differentiate it from the Jewish covenant. We have already seen above that Jesus called for the observance of the Law (Torah), even though at times he interpreted it differently. As James Parkes writes, "He [Jesus] did not reject the idea of interpreting the Law, for He interpreted it freely Himself, but He did reject some of their actual interpretations, and refused to give 'their traditions' the force of Torah itself."[3] Moreover, Christianity was different from the teaching of Jesus. For example, this was evident in the meaning that Paul assigned to the death and resurrection of Jesus. Reducing the status and even eliminating the Law and substituting faith for it, as well as elevating Adam's disobedience to a necessary prerequisite for the Christian faith, thus making it a permanent condition of man, that of a sinner, represented much of the essential difference.

Let us first consider the reduction of the status of the Law, since this was the main cause for the separation of the two faiths and, in my view, is mainly responsible for the possibility of the Holocaust. Paul himself actually realized that his abandonment of the Law represented a paradox, because the Law, as he claims, does not save but nevertheless must have been an integral part of God's overall plan. Paul tried to answer this by claiming that God gave the Law so that the Jews could sin and therefore have the need for Jesus. This, however, presents another problem. If the Gentiles can be saved by God through Jesus, why would God select the Jews to make them slaves of sin by giving the Torah to them, thus requiring God to sacrifice His Son to redeem the Jews? This is completely incomprehensible on the part of a God of wisdom. The Jews could not have been guilty of sin because of the Law, since their actions were not volitional or free, inasmuch as their actions were a part of God's plan. Why not send Jesus before the giving of the Law and thus save all people equally? God could have sent Jesus earlier, at the time of Sodom and Gomorrah or at the time of the Flood, when evil was very prevalent. Why would He want to wait to give the Torah, which, according to Paul, demanded the sacrifice of His Son to save the world? The economy of salvation is significantly absent in the situation. To eliminate this paradox, one must assume that Jesus was not sent to eliminate the Law, as indeed Jesus himself states in Matthew, as cited before.

Paul realized that if the Law saved, then Jesus died in vain. It was, therefore, necessary for Paul to address this problem. His solution was to replace the substance of the Hebrew Bible with faith in Jesus, a new covenant of faith. As a result of this move, the relational status of the people Israel was abrogated. Paul's claim is radically weakened, however, by the fact that God, being God, cannot abrogate a covenant; such action would introduce problems of arbitrariness on the part of God so that the Christian covenant itself could also be changed in the future. These implications extend to theological readings of modern history as well. Thus the involuntary dispersion of the Jews, which in the Christian view was the result of God's condemnation of the Jews for rejecting Jesus and for the charge of deicide, was ended by the reestablishment of the state of Israel. If we were to accept Paul's logic, then the place of the Jews has been, in fact, restored. Paul's thesis thus fails.

Christian theology refers to the Law as remaining unfulfilled in the old covenant and conceives of the new covenant as providing its ultimate fulfillment. The reason the old covenant is unfulfilled, Christianity claims, is simply that man is incapable of fulfilling the Law. What is required, therefore, is the transformation of man into a being capable of being placed in an authentic salvific relation to God. Furthermore, Paul claimed that the nonfulfillment of the Law is due to the very content of the Law, this in spite of the previously cited passages of Matthew. Paul claimed: "All that the Law can do is to make man conscious of sin" (Romans 3:20). Is the consciousness of sin a bad thing? And the people who were not under the Law, didn't they ever sin? "If it had not been for the Law, I should never have learned what sin was . . . for sin is lifeless without law" (Romans 7:7–8). The example he uses is "you must not covet," which "led me to all sorts of covetous ways" (Romans 7:7–8). This may be interpreted to mean that if there were no "Law," he could covet and not have it considered a sin. Bringing this to its logical conclusion, one could commit all kinds of evil acts and not sin, because the Law is no longer operative.

Paul makes a gross error in stating that "sin is lifeless without law." What makes man conscious of sin is the knowledge of the difference between good and evil. If Paul had been conscious of that difference, he would "not covet" irrespective of whether that law was prescribed or not. The idea that a moral law ("you must not covet") should have led Paul to "all sorts of covetous ways" or "evil ways" is totally without foundation and contradictory.

Paul called the Law a "curse" from which Christ ransomed humans by taking the "curse" upon himself (Galatians 3:13). By this action, God sacrified His own Son. Paul claimed that the

Law does not rest on faith. By contrast, Jewish tradition considered the event at Sinai, when God offered the Torah and the Jewish people said, "We will *do* and we will *listen,*" to be an unparalleled act of faith.

The old covenant is seen by the Christians as concerned with the external behavior of men, which is only a part of man's life. This criticism is unjust because, in the Jewish view, it is precisely through the behavior of man that the God-man relationship is realized. While the Christian covenant may apply to some external acts of man, it is mainly the inner intention that is important to Christianity, because this gives rise to the spiritual dimension. The basic concern of Christianity is the vertical element of the covenant, which *neutralizes the horizontal element, which is of such import to the Jewish view, and which results in the elimination of man-to-man responsibility.* Essentially, what is at stake here is Christianity's replacement of deed by the concept of creed. To put it differently, Christianity preaches the redemption of man from the world of sin, while Judaism urges the redemption of this world from sin through the action of man.

A Christian can achieve individual salvation through faith alone, irrespective of his behavioral pattern (whosoever believes in Jesus has eternal life). A Jew, through his deeds, contributes to the redemption of the community and the world, not to individual salvation. While Paul does not minimize the importance of good behavior, it is his judgment that this is only a derivative of faith. Paul's teachings of man's freedom from the Law gave man the license to practice unethical behavior. Paul's doctrine of Grace, through the expiatory death of Christ, seemed to the Jews to strike at the root of all morality, by paralyzing the human will. Albert Schweitzer observed: "Paul arrives at the idea of a faith which rejects not only the works of the Law, but works in general. He thus closes the pathway to a theory of ethics."[4]

Faith in Jesus that brings salvation does not promote responsibility in man (i.e., in the sense of prior responsibility before the act). Law does. Faith is not sufficient to guarantee justice and does not inculcate good morals, because immoral acts are found forgiven in the faith itself, in the atoning death of Jesus—that is to say, "there was virtually no such thing as a distinctive Christian moral system. What was distinctive is that such ethical instruction as it offered was now linked, not with the Torah or any code dependent on it, but with Christ."[5] I may add that such ethical instructions were based on Jesus' teachings that were Jewish but were not emphasized. Grant further states:

> . . . the real novelty of Christianity, then, was not any system of good conduct, but the new *motive* it supplies for this: namely, the motive deduced from God's revelatory action through Jesus Christ. This, to Paul, was important; the good conduct would follow from it. Paul looks to the inspiration of Christ to make the fruits of the spirit flower in the soul. Where, then, is there a need for a code of conduct?[6]

Furthermore, the Christian view of man as a sinner and of this world as only a vestibule for the greater bliss of an afterlife with Jesus, an eschatological view, contrasts crucially with the Jewish emphasis of this life as the most important basis for the redemptive messianic age to become a reality (the horizontal element). Since Christianity's fundamental vision of man is that of "Fallen Man," the Christian becomes subject to this condition without hope of overcoming it by his own efforts. To overcome this, a countersymbol had to be established, which is baptism, an act of Grace, through which man's original condition is nullified and man is purified. Baptism, however, does not change man's nature. The effect of baptism on Christians has not been borne out in history.

Christianity lost sight of the revelatory sense of community demonstrated at Sinai, since it separated itself from the synagogue. The Church's interpretation of the Christ event became more and more individualistic in the negative sense of the term.

It turned to an I-God relationship in which people believed they could reach full communion with God without achieving communion with the rest of humanity. The result was a *loss of responsibility for the human family*. Christianity had lost sight of that notion of salvation that is ultimately communal. The difference in the two religious views of the covenant made the Holocaust a possibility, if not an inevitability. *The difference between the faiths represents a necessary, but not sufficient, cause.* Without the Christian view of limiting the covenant to the vertical element and eliminating the importance of the horizontal element, the Holocaust could not have happened. Through its omission of the teaching of the moral relationship and social obligations of justice among humans as a necessary religious duty, an omission that is implicit in the Christian view of the covenant, the latter promoted an indifference to and even cooperation with retrograde forces culminating in the Holocaust.

The Nazi disruption of Western traditions did not sweep over Europe out of a vacuum; its antecedents lay in German history and its portents in post–World War I literature. Friedrich Nietzsche wrote: "I foresee something terrible. Chaos everywhere. Nothing left which is of any value, nothing which commands: 'Thou shalt!' " He and others predicted the moral nihilism of the twentieth century, the revolt against reason and the limitless pursuit of the irrational. Nazi Germany materialized the progression toward this chaos. What remains is the hope that man will accept the partnership concept with God, which will reverse the condition of the world.

In this covenantal sense, the Holocaust presents a challenge to Christianity far greater than that it presents to Judaism. The Holocaust happened in the center of Christian Europe and was perpetrated by Christians. Even in 1944, as the war was nearing its end, a papal nuncio is reported to have said: "There is no innocent blood of Jewish children in the world. All Jewish blood is guilty. You have to die. This is the punishment that has been awaiting you because of deicide."[7]

The unwillingness of the Church to censure such spokesmen during the Holocaust and its failure, even after the Holocaust, to repent of their role—that is to say, the role of the Church itself—must be carefully considered. Part of these considerations will have to include the ambiguities surrounding Church policy on the question of activism in different arenas of conflict, e.g., Poland on the one hand and Latin America on the other.

Franklin H. Littell states: "The truth about the murder of European Jewry by baptized Christians is this: it raises in a most fundamental way the question of the credibility of Christians. Was Jesus a false Messiah? No one can be a true Messiah whose followers feel compelled to torture and destroy other human persons who think differently."[8]

The two major factors principally responsible for a Christian theological reappraisal, popularly described as post-Holocaust theology, were the feelings of guilt about the Christian complicity in the Holocaust and the re-creation of the state of Israel. According to Paul Van Buren, " . . . neither of these two events, the Holocaust and the existence of the state of Israel, standing alone could have caused such a change. Only when the shock of horror of the Holocaust was coupled with the other, even greater theological shock of the existence of the Jewish state, do we begin to see the first reversals of the church's teachings about the Jews."[9] That Israel's existence is the greater shock to traditional Christian theology, even beyond the feeling of guilt about the Holocaust, derives from Christian teachings that the Jews were dispersed and abandoned by God when they refused to regard Jesus as the Messiah. The reemergence of the state of Israel is a direct negation of that claim; hence, the necessity for a reevaluation of Christian theology, especially in recognition that Judaism ceased to be a fossilized relic. The assertion that the Church replaced the Jews as the Chosen People now comes to be seen as an untenable argument that contained in it genocidal implications. Any Christian who speaks to a Jew today must do so fully aware that it was his tradition that contributed greatly to create the Holocaust.

While it is generally recognized that Christianity did not invent anti-Semitism, the Church certainly developed anti-Semitism for its own purposes to its highest level of justification. What Paul and the entire Christian tradition taught is unmistakably negative: the religion of Judaism is now superseded, the Torah abrogated, the promises fulfilled in the Christian Church, the Jews struck with blindness, and whatever remains of the election of Israel rests as a burden upon them in the current age.[10] The masses of the Christian people became thoroughly inculcated with this deeply ingrained teaching about the Jew, which provided the foundation Hitler could use to legitimize his purpose: to exterminate the Jewish people.

At the very beginning of Christianity, when the Temple fell, the idea took hold that this was a sign of God's punishment of the Jewish people for rejecting Jesus. (Compare this to the Jewish concept of this event, which related to the horizontal element of the covenant.) The Jew became the condemned eternal wanderer, despised by God and guilty of deicide. The mark of Cain was upon him. The Jews were the children of the Devil, and they were evil. For Christianity to establish its own church and to show its superiority, Judaism had to be denigrated and perceived as controlled by Satan.

The historic statements of church leaders, including popes and leaders such as Chrysostom and Augustine, were a continuous litany claiming the evil and perfidy of the Jews. The programs advocated to eliminate the Jewish evil consisted of vicious sequences of evil deeds. The words of Martin Luther bear repeating in this context as well:

Jews want to rule the world and already dominate many good Christians; they are arch-criminals, killers of Christ and Christendom; they are a plague, pestilence and pure misfortune.

Among his remedies are:

. . . burning synagogues, burning Jewish homes, since in these Judaism is practiced; confiscating religious books; prohibiting rabbis the teaching of Judaism on the pain of death; prohibiting Jewish travel; prohibiting Jewish moneylending and confiscating gold and silver.[11]

Christian teachings and nineteen centuries of being raised in the culture of Fallen Man (the fundamental vision of man in Christianity), in addition to the fact that creed, not Law, was the most important factor for salvation, became one of the foundations for Shoah by preparing the masses for such an event. Christianity's teaching that the world is only a vestibule for the next world, where one is with Jesus, in contradistinction to the Jewish view that life in this world is the important consideration for redemption, added to the process of denigrating the man-man facet of the covenant and thus contributed to the possibility of the Holocaust.

The occurrence of the Holocaust can be traced to the convergence of several elements. The crucial element lies in the Christian view of the covenant as contrasted to the Jewish view. Judaism's view consists of a vertical relationship (God-man), which is refracted in the horizontal (man-man) relationship. The Christian view consists essentially of the vertical view (God-man). Creed is the essential factor, not deed, as in Judaism. What is important to the Christian is personal salvation that is achieved by faith only and not social commitment. Without the horizontal component, the man-man relationship can degenerate into radical evil. The theological anti-Semitism of the Church helped to prepare the foundation of the Holocaust.

Notes

1. Isaac Husik, *A History of Medieval Jewish Philosophy* (Philadelphia, PA: Jewish Publication Society, 1940), pp. 162–63.
2. Paul Ramsey, "Elements of a Biblical Political Theory," *Journal of Religion* 29, no. 5 (1949): 258.
3. James Parkes, *Conflict of the Church and Synagogue* (New York: Atheneum, 1981), p. 45.
4. As quoted by Michael Grant in *Saint Paul* (New York: Charles Scribner, 1976), p. 97.
5. Ibid.
6. Ibid.
7. Quoted by Irving Greenberg in "Judaism and Christianity after the Holocaust," *Journal of Ecumenical Studies* 12 (Fall 1975), pp. 525–26.
8. Franklin H. Littell, *The Crucifixion of the Jew* (New York: Harper and Row, 1975), p. 17.
9. Quoted in Henry Friedlander and Sybil Milton, *The Holocaust: Ideology, Bureaucracy, and Genocide* (New York: Kraus International Publications, 1980), p. 286.
10. Rosemary Reuter, *Faith and Fratricide: The Theological Roots of Anti-Semitism* (New York: Seabury, 1979), p. 6.
11. Cited by Franklin H. Littell in *The Crucifixion of the Jews* (New York: Harper and Row, 1975), p. 105.

PART C

The Resolution of the Problem of Suffering and Evil Leading to a New Theology as Well as a Theodicy

The existence of evil remains an unanswered question. Despite millennial efforts to address it, none has proven satisfactory. The concepts developed in Section A point to a theologically fruitful way of dealing with this question.

Chapter XII
The Problem of Suffering and Evil in the Theological Tradition

No other problem of theology, especially in modern times, has excited so sustained and wide an interest as the problem of suffering. Suffering poses a problem for religion particularly, insofar as it seems to contradict the notion of an all-powerful, perfect, benevolent God. Judaism has attempted to cope with the problem of suffering in various ways, principally in terms of retributive theodicy or punishment for sin.

The most formidable challenge to such theodicies arises where suffering of the innocent and the prosperity of the wicked are conjoined. The traditional response to this challenge has turned on the doctrine of reward and punishment in the afterlife: the righteous suffer in this world even for the little evil they may have done in order to receive their reward in the afterworld; the evil obtain their reward in this world for the good they may have done in order to receive punishment in the afterworld.[1]

Medieval Jewish philosophers frequently distinguish between two kinds of evil that befall man—moral and physical. Moral evils include those actions that people willfully inflict upon each other—robbery, murder, war, rape, abuse of children, exploitation, etc. To this we would also add religious persecution and race hatred. They are functions of free will. Physical evils afflict man from outside sources, such as floods, earthquakes, hurricanes, tornadoes, and diseases. Here free will is not involved.

In the beginning of Nathaniel West's short novel, *Miss Lonelyhearts*, a girl who is born without a nose asks whether she should commit suicide in view of the unspeakable suffering resulting from deformity. This sorry state should not be considered an evil. In general, medical problems—a child born dead or deformed either physically or mentally—are not evil in themselves; they are a result of causes still unknown to man. Physiology should not be identified with God. Also, there is no need to search for "deeper" explanations for drought or other onslaughts of nature in defense of God. Nature is not law to be followed; it is power to be controlled.

The rabbis generally seek explanations for suffering that free God from the possibility of indictment by man. If man suffers, there is a good reason. "If a man sees that painful suffering visit him, let him examine his conduct" (B'rakhot 5a); and "There is no death without sin and no suffering without transgression" (Shabbat 55B). If self-examination fails to reveal a man's moral failure, let him attribute his suffering to the neglect of the study of Torah. Moreover, even if he is a diligent student, he may attribute his pain to God's "chastisement of love."

The medieval religious philosophers tried to vindicate God's role in physical evils. Augustine formulated the classic philosophical view of evil, which states that since everything that exists must have been created by God and, therefore, must be good, evil is not an existent, but is merely privation, i.e., the absence of good. But privation itself is an evil, for the world is then not complete. This essentially neoplatonic doctrine also has a long tradition in Jewish philosophy. Maimonides, being among those who adopted this view, claims that matter, which by nature is always a concomitant of privation, must be regarded as the cause of all corruption and evil. In accordance, Maimonides also claimed that "no evil can descend from on high," for only goodness resides in God. (There is a similarity here to the Christian concept that the soul is good and the body [matter] is the source of all evil.) I find this paradoxical in that matter, being a creation of God, must be good and, therefore, cannot be a concomitant of privation.

The theory of privation is not a satisfactory explanation for evil. God created everything, which, therefore, must be good. Privation depends on man's creativity and activity. With the development of technology, blindness is no longer the absence of sight; with the proper instruments, blind men can see; darkness is not the absence of light as a result of the development of intrared instruments by the use of which we see in the darkness. It is man who is responsible for the elimination of evil effects of natural phenomena and conditions (see 1:28).

Another criticism of the theory of privation is that it refuses to recognize the binary character of existence. If evil is the absence of good, dishonesty is the absence of honesty, death is the absence of life, impiety is the absence of piety, weakness is the absence of strength, sickness is the absence of health, etc. While each of the above is true within itself, nevertheless, both sides of each statement actually exist and are part of our experience. The world cannot exist without both characteristics. Indeed, without evil, theism would not have emerged, for evil is a necessary prerequisite of theism. Without evil, there would be no forgiveness, no compassion, no reward or punishment. The binary system is necessary for life to exist.

There is a third element that represents indifference or a neutral position, which is actually the zero point of transition from the positive feature of a characteristic to the negative side. But this condition is not stable, because any variance of a factor throws the unstable condition to either side. The exploration of the reason for the world existing in a binary functional system may be found in Genesis in the introduction of the Tree of Knowledge of Good and Evil. In the broadest meaning of good and evil, God made them a part of the texture of nature. Otherwise, God would not mention *knowledge* of good and evil. Knowledge presupposes the existence of the object of knowledge. In the introduction of the Tree of Life and subsequent expulsion of Adam, the mortality of man was introduced and emphasized, which also expresses the binary form of our existence.

The problem of suffering demands our attention. There are at least three ways of addressing this question. If we accept the position that everything is due to chance, the question is answered a priori. However, if the why of suffering asks for a purpose, a proximate cause will not do. A second solution may be offered. If we say that the universe, far from being governed by chance, is subject to ironclad laws, but not to any ultimate purpose, the problem of suffering is again taken care of. Third, if we assume that the world is governed by purpose, we need only add that this purpose is not especially intended to prevent suffering.

The theological problem of suffering becomes perplexing once certain presuppositions are accepted. These are: God is omnipotent and God is just and good. As long as these assumptions are granted, this problem may not be solved or may be difficult to solve. Traditional theism is never adequately defensible in the face of suffering.

Man calls death a destructive evil. Maimonides shows how metaphysical wisdom can offer its own solace with respect to death. Such a misleading error could be avoided, would we but understand. "In accordance with the divine wisdom, genesis can only take place through destruction, and without destruction of the individual members of the species, the species themselves would not exist permanently."[2]

To the question of how could a loving, powerful God have allowed the Holocaust, the ultimate evil, to happen, which involved children and righteous men, Buber answers through the use of the biblical concept of *hester panim*—that God hid his face. In other words, God is eclipsed or hidden, obscured by the extent and intensity of evil in the world.[3] This would indicate either that God hid His face (a metaphor using an anthropomorphic expression) to allow the evil to happen or that the hiddenness was imposed on Him by the intensity of evil. If hiding His face is a voluntary action, God's omnipotence or goodness is put in jeopardy. Either He does not care to or is unable to intervene, or the people deserved the punishment (according to the covenant). However, no one deserves the radicality of evil Auschwitz inflicted. Furthermore, why would God "hide His face" from the Jews of Europe only? God being universal, we would expect His actions to apply universally, not just to Europe. Certainly, if "hiding His face" were operative, the Jews in the United States were more appropriate victims. After all, the cream of Judaism was in Europe, not in the United States. The position of God's "hiding his face" is also subject to questions: *What is the proper duration of God's hiddenness? At what point is "the cry of the innocent blood" of a suffering people "heard by God?"* Does hester panim *apply to communities or individuals?* It seems to apply to communities only, in view of conditions at the times of Sodom and Gomorrah, before Noah or the city of Nineveh. (This shows that in *biblical times* God's actions applied to communities only.)

Another explanation for the silence of God, in Cabalistic terms, is *tsimtsum,* where God contracts himself to give man more freedom to maneuver and the wicked more time to return to Him. I assume this applies only to Jews. This is a strange concept to invoke for our position, since in the case of the Holocaust and the Inquisition, the wicked ones were the Nazis and Inquisitors, respectively, not the Jews.

The history of Israel, fideistically viewed, is repeatedly plagued by the experience of God's hiddenness. God is both hidden and present, far and near, depending on circumstances. This is precisely the dilemma that faith in God presents. Generally speaking, the dilemma results from the assumption that righteousness ensures God's presence and wickedness His absence.

This is the classic interpretation of God's hiddenness.[4] It is man, then, who determines, by his free will, whether God remains present or goes into hiding. In the case of the Nazis, where the Jews were denied the exercise of their free will, the enormity of evil required God's justice to become manifest, not hidden. The disparity between religious convictions and the actual experience brought the issue to the forefront of Jewish thought.

The concept of a "challenging" God contrasts with the concept of a "commanding" God.[5] The challenging God demands a choice from man, the use of the free will with which he was created. Choice is the central issue for man. It determines what man becomes. Man is the result of a continuum of choices. The Bible is full of references to "choose good." In accepting God's challenge to become responsible for the condition of this world, man becomes a partner of God and then discharges the responsibility of existence with responsible freedom because his decision stems from his own conviction and intellectual resolve not superimposed.

On the other hand, in the case of a "commanding" God, then by virtue of His commandments, which we must follow if we truly believe in Him, why did God create man with a free will? Man, in the absence of the power of choice, would then become an automaton who follows the commandments, but he would have no conception of their meaning and reasons thereof. There would be no progress in religion under such circumstances, but in having free will man can accept God and truly believe in or reject Him. Without free will, man's observances would be meaningless.

The statement that the making of some wrong choices is *logically necessary* for freedom to exist is wrong. Those who assert that free will requires the possibility of evil claim a logical necessity, but it is empirically false that man is always responsible for his own suffering. The Crusades, the Inquisition, the pogroms are examples of this. Second, the choices that are based on the individual's sense of responsible freedom need not be necessarily wrong. Some people may err in their choices, even when made with responsible freedom, but these errors are not logically necessary. If man is wholly and *absolutely* free (that is, he rejects God's assignment of responsibility), it would follow that he revolts against God, thus negating God's omnipotence. If, however, man chooses to become a partner of God in this world and assume the responsibility for this world, his choice expresses the will of God and thus the actions of his free will will be necessarily positive, not evil.

The concept of "everything is in the hands of Heaven except the fear of Heaven" is of interest here. Maimonides states (the Eight Chapters) that "fear is not in the hands of Heaven," but in the appetitive part of the soul. Indeed, it is given over to man's choice. Thus, in saying, "Everything is in the hands of Heaven," the sages mean the natural matters about which a man has no choice, such as his being tall or short, or a rainfall or drought, or the air being putrid or healthy, and so, too, with respect to everything in the world, except for the movement and the rest of man.

Even some natural occurrences may be transferred from the hands of Heaven to the province of man's choice, such as the condition of the air (man has control of air pollution). Drought could be eliminated by reforestation and by progress in science, etc. Thus it is man's responsibility to control all of earthly life for the benefit of mankind by more effort (1:28). Even hurricanes and typhoons may become subject to man's future control as science and technology advance. Of course, man will never be able to control the movement of the stars or the changes in the galaxies, but these have nothing to do with the quality of human life.

In order to complete the subject of suffering, it would be proper to discuss the views of some specific medieval philosophers and the views of some modern philosophers in the aftermath of the greatest gratuitious suffering that befell the Jewish people, the Holocaust.

According to Maimonides,

Three kinds of evil can befall mankind:

1. Evils that are a consequence of "coming-to-be" and "passing away" of that which is endowed with matter. These include natural phenomena that negatively affect human beings, such as earthquakes, floods and birth deformities. Since all material bodies are subject to degeneration and corruption, such evils are necessary for the perpetuation of the species. [How does death contribute to the perpetuation of the species?] Maimonides does not differentiate lives between fully lived and early death as the result of accidental occurrences.

2. Social evils that men inflict upon one another, such as war and violent crimes.

3. Those evils that an individual inflicts upon himself as a consequence of vice and bodily overindulgence.[6]

The question of what is the correlation of God, omnipotent and good, and the three kinds of evil becomes inescapable. Maimonides claimed that the misfortunes (the third kind of evil) inflicted by punishment are deserved[7] and therefore just. Are they not rather the results of man's excessive obsession, such as smoking and drinking, which are health hazards? Or the abuse of drugs, which is definitely an invitation to damage one's health?

Maimonides emphasized that he relied upon a "fundamental principle of the Law of Moses, our Master, that man has the absolute ability to do what he wills or chooses among the things concerning which he has the ability to act" and that "it is in no way possible that God should be unjust." Maimonides affirmed unconditionally that "all the calamities . . . and all the good things that come to man, be it a single individual or a group, are all of them determined according to the deserts of man . . . in which there is no injustice whatever." Maimonides even considered that any pain, however minute, can be no other than a divine punishment. Does he insist that volcanic eruptions or floods are deliberately caused to provide proper deserts for man? What if in the midst of such events are found men of saintly and intellectual characteristics?

Maimonides linked the problem of the fall of Adam with the citation above. He considered mortality punitive rather than natural and consistent with the biblical notion that death was the penalty inflicted upon Adam for his primal disobedience. Here he differs from the first of his arguments, in which he claimed that death is necessary for the survival of the species and therefore not punitive.

The second kind of evil can be found in classical Judaism in the idea of freely chosen disobedience of man. This is noticed in the conditional element of the covenant. The prophet was used as God's mouthpiece to remind Israel that the covenant was broken and to seek its restoration to wholeness. In normative Judaism, then, there is only one criterion of evil, which is rebellion against God or transgression of the covenant. In my view, this translates into rejection of God's assignment of responsibility of existence by man or, in different terminology, the rejection of man's partnership with God. (This will be discussed more fully later on when I will present my theology.)

The Holocaust speaks in the strongest voice the complete rejection of Maimonides's views as well as the normative views of Judaism. There is no way to claim that one and a half million children freely disobeyed God. The conditional elements of the covenant simply state that a good and satisfying life would result if God's commandments were followed, while a broken covenant would result in a life full of dire consequences. But this did not prevent suffering to befall Jews who maintained the covenant. These Jews fell victim to the pogroms, religious hate, intense false patriotic fervor against minority elements, etc. These situations are not consistent with the results one would expect from the observance of the ethical behavior demanded by covenant theology.

Crescas observes that the righteous do not deserve to suffer for their righteousness, and he maintains that the reward and punishment theory holds for the next world, but not for this world. Here he takes issue with Maimonides, who suggests that evil does not come from God directly, but by accident and by reason of matter.[8] However, since "matter is an evil necessary for the perpetuation of the species" and since death was God's punishment of Adam for disobedience, death is a necessary condition for life, with God as the cause of it.

As far as this world is concerned, Crescas makes other excuses, among which are that evil is sometimes a good in disguise, and vice versa; that sometimes one inherits evil and good from one's parents, not explaining the reasons why this occurs in certain cases only, etc. Evil in the moral sense does not come from God, but punishment does, and as its aim is justice, it is a good, not an evil. This is true only if the punishment is justified and bears a relation to the degree of moral evil.

But why did God have to punish all life—human, animal, and plant? If perpetuation of the species is important, the punishment by death was not a punishment, but a good. The trouble with such reasoning is that death is nearly always accompanied by suffering and misfortune. Thus the "good" is infected with evil, which is a necessary precondition of death. Who is responsible for this type of evil, if not God? Maimonides, however, claims that the misfortunes that befall individual men are the divinely inflicted punishment they deserve.[9] But since everyone is subject to death, the suffering prior to death cannot be punishment.

Abraham ibn Daud is subject to error in his attempt to uphold the theory that evil cannot be ascribed to God. Relying more on

Aristotelian logic than upon Scripture or tradition, he states that if both evil and good could emanate from God, there would be two contraries in the same subject at the same time, which is logically impossible. However, God created both good and evil as part of the texture of nature and then assigned the world to man. In this world, good and evil actions, then, depend on man's choices. Good and evil are not characteristics of God, even though they owe their existence to God's creation. This is no different from God creating solid or fluid things and then man claiming that they are a characteristic of God, or clouds, winds, earth, etc. Creation cannot be understood as being a part of God; God is outside nature, even though He is present in nature. Abraham ibn Daud claims that God cannot be the cause of both good and evil, for then He would be a composite being, like man, which is contrary to God's unity and simplicity. But God's assignment of this world to man would eliminate God's involvement in causing both good and evil, for this becomes man's province, for which possibility he was given free will.

Saadya declares unequivocally that God does not produce evil; he merely creates those things that are capable of becoming sources of well-being or evil through *man's own choice*. Saadya reflects the view held by Plato, who is likewise of the opinion that God is identified with the good, and that under no condition can God be regarded as producing evil. The evil that is present is to be attributed to the material. (But God also created the material and therefore it would be good.) Evil may spring from matter, the flesh or an inherited disposition.[10] Thus if man were to eat improper, excessive, or insufficient amounts of food and not of the proper quality, this would be considered an evil. He does not mention hate, religious persecution, etc., which cannot be attributed to matter.

I have cited the views of several medieval Jewish philosophers on the issue of good and evil. Every one of them considers that God is not and cannot be the originator of evil. However, there are several arguments that point in a different direction. In the Adam story, God plants a Tree of Knowledge of Good and Evil in the Garden of Eden. The mention of good and evil presupposes their existence; otherwise no mention of them could be made. The presence of good and evil meant simply that they already belonged to the texture of nature that God created; otherwise God would refer to the Tree of Good and Evil only, not specifying knowledge of them. Simlarly, the punishment of death. It likewise was already a part of the texture of nature and Maimonides's argument becomes contradictory here. Since Adam was already material, consisting of flesh at the time of the test, he was subject to deterioration and death in order for the continuity of species to be possible. Adam was thus consigned to death before the punishment. Thus the threat of death was not really a threat at all.

As for the the problem of why the righteous suffer and the evil prosper, no satisfactory answer is forthcoming. It is shunted aside to a nebulous world beyond. If the soul is the only thing left after death and the body decomposes completely, how would the person be given his due reward and punishment?

What about the source of evil? Medieval thought advances the idea that matter or flesh is the source and that God created things that are capable of becoming the sources of evil through man's own choice. Maimonides says: "Matter is the concomitant of evil." This cannot be true, as pointed out before, because matter was created by God for a purpose and, therefore, must be good.

We shall now examine some modern Jewish philosophers' views on suffering in the aftermath of the Holocaust.

In 1966, Richard Rubenstein's book, *After Auschwitz,* broke the theological silence on the question of the meaning of the Holocaust, which represents the absolute evil:

> Although Jewish history is replete with disaster, none has been as radical in its total impact as the Holocaust. Our images of God,

man and the moral order have been permanently impaired. No Jewish theology will possess even a remote degree of relevance to contemporary Jewish life if it ignores God and the death camps. That is *the question* for Jewish theology in our times. Regrettably, most attempts at formulating a Jewish theology since World War II seems to have been written as if the decisive events in our time for Jews, the death camps and the birth of Israel had not taken place.[11]

Rubenstein's understanding (or lack of understanding) of the radicality of the Holocaust led him to state:

I reached a theological point of no return: if I believed in God as the omnipotent author of the historical drama and Israel as His Chosen People, I had to accept Dean Grüber's conclusion that it was God's will that Hitler committed six million Jews to slaughter. I could not possibly believe in such a God nor could I believe in Israel as the Chosen People of God after Auschwitz.[12]

The weakness in Rubenstein's position is his acceptance of Dean Grüber's conclusion that it was God's Will that Jews perished in the Holocaust, i.e., his uncritical acceptance of the underlying traditional view that sin is the cause of suffering. Rubenstein then suggests that even the suffering of one blameless child disproves the existence of the traditional God. Here, again, he makes a gross error. He fails to distinguish between suffering as a result of natural phenomena (which include illness) and the suffering inflicted by people who have rejected the assignment of responsibility by God. As a consequence, he substitutes a nonpersonal God of nature. Rubenstein views God as the "source and life of nature," and "nature's inevitabilities are seen as part of the tragic course of existence itself, rather than as God's retaliation against human sinfulness."[13] This nonpersonal and nonhistorical God is incapable of being good or evil.

Fackenheim answers the question: "If God intervened at the Exodus, why did He not do so at Auschwitz?" by defining Exodus as a root experience; it produced a nation. As a root experience, it is unique. The implication is that God intervenes only in such unique events, but the rest of the time He withdraws (an absent God), leaving everything in the hands of man.

Berkovits claims that God, in granting man freedom of choice, must demonstrate His patience with the wicked, which in a way shows God's "mightiness." This demonstration of His power in the world would not be a great accomplishment, Berkovits claims, but controlling the use of His infinite power is a manifestation of real strength.[14] Is God more interested in demonstrating His real strength than in helping the suffering of His Chosen People? If God has been directing the political process, why did He prolong the suffering of the Jewish people? With this restraint during the Holocaust, God gave to men and nations the opportunity to act justly, but God has been directing the political process so that the nations finally saw the light and chose to oppose Hitler and then defeat him, even though initially they left the Jews to the designs of Hitler. One might think that the nations went to war against Hitler for the sake of the Jewish people. This is poor history and poor interpretation of the events. It is also poor theology bordering on the obscene, because it requires the sacrifice of innocent and righteous people for the sake of hope for the sinners' return. Why were there so many nations and people helping Hitler to the very end with the elimination of the Jews? Why did not the "nations who chose to get involved" do so much earlier in view of *Mein Kampf*? Why did the Allies decide not to bomb the camps of annihilation? Why were the people on the the ship *St. Louis* turned away? Millions of Jewish lives could have been saved. Yet Berkovits can claim "that it did not become the Final Solution as was planned by the powers of darkness enables the Jew who has known of divine presence intimations of familiar concern [to what extent] in the midst of abandonment."[15]

Ignatz Maybaum uses the failure of the Final Solution, the fact that a remnant has survived, as being in harmony with Isaiah's prophecy "a remnant shall return." Six million Jews, one-third of the Jewish people, representing even a much higher ratio of the leadership, the learned, intellectual, spiritual, artistic, and scientific strata of Judaism's best, perished and Maybaum claims that the remnant, in view of the failure of the Final Solution, represents as great a miracle as happened at the Red Sea.[16]

Why could not God have intervened at a much smaller ratio than a third? Hitler's destruction of the Jews occurred only in countries he controlled. There could not be a Final Solution unless he conquered the United States and other free nations. This was the only reason for the largest portion of the remnant. Even dictators have the power of restraint. Why did God's patience with the wicked last so long while, in the interim, many righteous people suffered and died? This represents a horrible argument and could easily justify Rubenstein's option for the denial of God in the face of the utter senselessness of the Holocaust.

In addition to the Jewish theologians and philosophers, there were many Christian philosophers who were very much concerned with the problem of good and evil. It was stated in three propositions:

1. God exists and is omnipotent.
2. God is wholly good.
3. Evil exists.

The question for the philosophers revolves around whether the proposition "God exists" is logically compatible with the proposition that evil exists. Hume argues that the two propositions are incompatible.[17] Yet, in a sense, evil is a necessary prerequisite for theism. If all evil were eradicated or nonexistent, would there be any necessity for God and redemption of man—a messianic world where the lamb would lie down with the wolf and not be afraid?

In dialogue II, Hume retreats somewhat from his strict position. He claims that even if "God exists" and "evil exists" are compatible propositions, the fact that the latter is true provides good reason (though no longer conclusive) for maintaining that the former is false.

Theologians have assumed that the question, "If there be a God, whence is the presence of so many evils?" is a valid question that necessitates attempts to provide answers. Leibniz held that the world God created is the best of all possible worlds. Each instance of evil contributes to the perfection of the world as a whole, even though this may be difficult to understand. If Hume's argument is correct, then any attempt to provide theodicies must be defective. Nevertheless, I shall present in the last two chapters an explanation that absolves God of any part in evil actions. Evil does not exist independently. It has meaning only in connection with an action and the timing of an event. If a man dies at the age of one hundred, we cannot possibly consider it an evil; if a man dies in his youth, we are predisposed to consider it evil.

Notes

1. However, in ancient Israel we find no concern with the afterlife whatever: for Moses, death is the end, and it is only in the very latest passages of the Bible, in Hellenic times, that we find a few intimations of immortality.
2. Maimonides, *Guide to the Perplexed*, 3:12.
3. Martin Buber, *The Prophetic Faith* (New York: Harper and Row, 1949), p. 191.
4. Deuteronomy 31:17, 32:18, 32:20; Isaiah 8:17, 54:8, 59:2, 64:6; Jeremiah 33:15; Job 13:24, 34:29.
5. Emil L. Fackenheim, *God's Presence in History* (New York: Harper and Row, 1972), pp. 14, 15, 95.
6. Maimonides, *Guide to the Perplexed*, 3:12.
7. Ibid.

8. Isaac Husic, *A History of Medieval Jewish Philosophy* (New York: Athenium, 1976), p. 394.
9. Maimonides, *Guide to the Perplexed*, 3:12.
10. Henry Blumberg, "Theories of Evil in Medieval Jewish Philosophy," *Hebrew Union College Annual*, 1972
11. Richard Rubenstein, *After Auschwitz* (Indianapolis: Bobbs-Merril, 1966), p. x.
12. Ibid., p. 46.
13. Ibid., pp. 135, 139.
14. Eliezer Berkovits, *Faith after the Holocaust* (New York: KTAV, 1973), p. 109.
15. Ibid., pp. 134–136.
16. Ignatz Maybaum, *The Face of God After Auschwitz* (Amsterdam: Polnk and Van Genup, 1965), p. 32.
17. David Hume, *Dialogues Concerning Natural Religion,* ed. H. D. Aiken (New York: Hefner, 1955), Dialogue 10.

Chapter XIII

An Analysis of Job: The Problem of Universality and Particularity in the Book of Job

In part A, chapter V, Abraham was observed acting as a partner of God because he demonstrated responsible commitment to the partnership. First, he questioned God on the issue of justice even for total strangers. Second, he resolved the questions of the sacrifice of Isaac without doing violence to his sense of justice and his faith in God. Job, on the other hand, exhibits an attitude in contrast to Abraham.

The character of Job as outlined in the Bible describes a man with no sense of communal responsibility. His challenge to God is limited to his own personal needs. Moreover, *Job* portrays its protagonist as suffering because of divine injustice, the result of a casual bet between God and Satan. Yet Job's narrow self-interest undermines the moral challenge against God in the Book of Job, which is considered a powerful universal work.

The Book of Job poses three intertwined issues: God's justice, human responsibility, and personal suffering. Job, like Abraham, cries out for divine justice. However, there the similarity ends. While Abraham demands God's justice on behalf of strangers in the cities of Sodom and Gomorrah, exhibiting a communal responsibility, Job argues on his own behalf, when suffering befalls him. Job, in further contrast to Abraham, complains that *his* suffering is undeserved and thus unjust. Job's complaint of injustice also sharply contrasts with Abraham, who does not complain but silently sets out to sacrifice his only son by his own hands. After much deliberation and anxiety and without asking God for an explanation of the demand, Abraham acts as a partner of God.

Nevertheless, since the terrible suffering that befalls Job is the result of a wager between God and the Adversary and not brought on by deliberate evil doing, it is undeserving. Unaware of the source of his trouble, Job claims that as a man of integrity and righteousness, his suffering is undeserved because "there is no suffering without sin."

From the very beginning of the prologue, Job is said to be "blameless and upright; he feared God and shunned evil" (Job 1:8).[1] This characterization does not necessarily place him on a high moral plane of responsibility. The Hebrew words מרע וסר ("turns away from evil") do not imply any responsibility on his part to actively *prevent* evil. This is confirmed in his relations with his children. When his children held feasts involving excessive drinking (Job 1:4,13),[2] instead of using his authority to prevent such actions,[3] which lend themselves to error,[4] Job "would send word to them to sanctify themselves" and he would make burnt offerings for each one of his children.

Job did little to prohibit or dissuade these revelries. Evidently, he was not concerned with actions that could result in spiritual and moral deficiencies, not even his children's. Job was guilty of acts of omission, not commission, although he helped the needy, the poor, the widows, the orphans, and the strangers.

As for Job's suffering, the prologue to the Book of Job continues with the conversation between God and the Adversary about Job. The Adversary argues with God: "Does Job not have good reason to fear God? But lay Your hand upon all that he has and he will surely blaspheme You." God agrees to a test. The question arises as to why God allows Himself to be challenged by the Adversary. Nachmanides's comment on Job 22:1 states:

"All trials in the Torah are for the benefit of the one being tested." If so, one may question of what possible benefit was this test to Job? It is apparently for the benefit of the Adversary, who has to be proved wrong. However, not every individual who finds himself in the same situation as Job will react as he did, since this is a subjective reaction, not an objective one. Thus Job represents a specific individual situation. The question itself, however, can be universalized in its application. Why do righteous people suffer? And it is to this question that we must eventually turn.

As for God's justice, God allows the Adversary to take the lives of Job's children. This is highly immoral. Why, in order to prove a point to the Adversary, is it necessary to take innocent lives (innocent in the sense of not being a principal in the test) ? Even in the test of Abraham, Isaac was spared. In this case, it was God who authorized the test. Also, in all other tests, it was God who initiated them, while in the case of Job He assigns the test to another party. This is a perplexing mystery.

Job's reaction to his suffering is inconsistent. He proclaims that "the Lord has given and the Lord has taken away, blessed be the name of the Lord" (Job 2:9), thus acknowledging God's unquestioned power and judgment. Yet he demands an explanation for God's actions. These statements exclude the right to question God, for they serve as the answer as well. If God gives possessions and health to a person, He has the sovereign right to take them away without being challenged for an explanation. We may refer to Rashi (Genesis 1:1) in this regard, who claims that since God as the Master of the world is the source of all creation, He can give the land to whomever He pleases. Thus Job does not utter any blasphemy with his lips against God, but he does lament and curse the day of his birth. If Job trusts God and everything that occurs is the result of God's will, his curses can easily be construed as blaming God. Job further complains that "the earth is given to evil and the cloud covers the face of the judge" (Job 9:24). However, since Job did not raise this complaint when he was well off on behalf of those less fortunate, he thus appears as indifferent and uncommitted, with no sense of responsibility beyond himself.

Modern commentators are sharply divided as to what the author of Job intended to teach his readers. The problem arises from the fact that in the speeches of God from the whirlwind (chapters 38–42), God ignores the issue as Job posed it. Job, in his own view a righteous person of integrity, challenges God for an explanation of his suffering. He sees only injustice in his situation. While he agrees with the concept that righteousness brings rewards and suffering is a result of sin, he denies that his suffering is a consequence of sin, as his three friends, Eliphaz, Bildad the Shuhite, and Zopher the Noamathite, insist. The implication is that Job's repeated assertions of a lack of a visible correlation between his life of rectitude and the dreadful fate visited upon him refutes his friends' contention that suffering is proof of sin.

Job, in ignorance of the reason for his suffering,[5] demands a confrontation with God and an explanation. God, however, cannot provide an explanation because Job's dreadful fate was a result of a wager with the Adversary. Instead of explaining Job's suffering, God confronts Job with a series of seemingly irrelevant, ironic questions intended to show him the paltriness of human knowledge and power. God's answer implies that it is presumptuous of man to question His justice, an answer that stands in sharp contrast to His patient answers to Abraham. Nevertheless, it is in the absence of any charge of guilt against Job in God's reply that one may find divine vindication of both Job's innocence and his argument, even though God did not affirm that there is suffering without sin.

God's constant reference to His awesome celestial power in answer to Job's desire for an explanation of the moral deficiency of justice in his innocent suffering leads to the conclusion, abhorrent in its nature, that "might makes right." Job, however, in finally encountering God in the whirlwind, stating, "This is my desire—that the Almighty answer me" (Job 31:35), makes the choice to continue to trust God, not because of His power, but because of His "Living Presence." God's appearing as a "Living Presence" to Job as an individual is not equivalent to God's appearing to the Jewish people at Sinai. God speaks to Job but does not answer his question. The author of Job cannot have God answer Job in view of the secret pact involving Job's suffering. Thus Job, in his ignorance of the cause of his suffering, can submit and in his defeat can say, "Even though He slay me, yet will I trust Him" (Job 13:15).

The Book of Job not only sustains the force of God's power, but points out that man is evil. All the protagonists in the book claim that man is evil. According to Biblical teaching, God implanted a *yetzer tov* and a *yetzer hara* in man. It is up to man to choose the *yetzer tov,* which is the bedrock of biblical ethics (Deuteronomy 30:16–19): "Behold, I have placed before you life and the good, and death and the evil . . . Life and death have I placed before you, the blessing and the curse: You shall choose life, so that you may live, you and your children." Eliphaz, Job's friend, denies that God's world order is the source of evil and places the blame squarely at the door of man:

> Indeed, misfortune does not come forth from the ground, nor does evil sprout from the earth. It is man who gives birth to evil . . .
> —Job 5:6–7

Job, in his bitter denial of his friend's position, never contravenes the moral responsibility of man. However, he demands the same standards from God. Based on the argument that God assigned the responsibility for the moral condition of the world to man (see part A, chapter III), Job, in demanding an answer from God with respect to his suffering, even though he claimed complete innocence, does not present a universal problem. He demanded to know why *he* personally suffered, not why suffering is present in the world created by a God of justice, love, and goodness. In the course of his speeches, however, he does refer to the broader problem. Since God challenged man to become responsible for the morality of the world, Job cannot address this question to God.

In the epilogue, Job's fortunes are restored and other children are born to him, as if one child can replace one that has been taken away. This situation certainly does not add to the theological and philosophical dialogues in the body of the book.

From our discussion, the Book of Job does not hold together as a theological or philosophical problem or solution. Even as a personal representation of a solution it fails, because of the conditions of the test on which the story was predicated.

Job's concern for himself (as indicated in the prologue regarding his children's parties) remains as such to the end—as seen in the "answer" that he gets and his willingness to submit to it. No reference to communal responsibility is mentioned at all. Job is satisfied with the return to his former state of being, rich and having children, but he does not instruct his children to avoid conditions that could lead to immoral behavior. He still believes that he is innocent and, therefore, suffering is not a consequence of sin. It is God's Will, which, within its wide, unlimited scope, includes the suffering of the innocent.

Notes

1. *The Book of Job* (Philadelphia: Jewish Publication Society, 1980).
2. A banquet (משתה) was so called from the prominence, at such feasts or banquets, of drinking, which led at times to excessive drunkenness. See *The International Critical Commentary—Job,* p. 6. "When a round of feast days was over" (Job 1:5) indicates that the feast was not an occasional event,

such as a birthday or a holiday. If they had been limited to one day's duration the book would not say: "This is what Job always used to do." (Job 1:5): (כל‌הימים), which denotes every day. The plural use of *days* indicates prolonged or frequent events.
3. "In ancient days, the children were regarded as the absolute property of their father." Robert Gordis, *The Book of Job, Commentary, New Translation—Special Studies* (New York: Jewish Theological Seminary of America, 1978), p. 2. Under these conditions, Job could have stopped these feasts.
4. As Job put it, "Perhaps my children have sinned and blasphemed God in their thoughts" (Job 1:5).
5. It is strange that Job, in view of all the various calamities happening in one day, considered these occurrences as a punishment by God and not as a test by God.

Chapter XIV
The Theological Resolution of the Problem of Evil: The Part Played by Man's Choice and Responsible Freedom

Human existence contains a tensional character. This tension arises from the fact that man belongs to two realms of existence: physical—that is, earthly existence manifested by man's desires of the flesh, self-interest, etc.—and the realm of spirituality and morality, which serves as a limit to the physical demands. In order to simplify the proposed solution of suffering and to present a theological model that resolves contradictions and inconsistencies, it is necessary to consider the two realms of man's existence separately. This is in line with the Torah's presentation in Genesis 1 and 2. Chapters I, II, and III in part A contain the detailed analyses and discussions that form the proposed solution.

Genesis 1 deals with the creation of the physical world. While God creates the world with the words: "Let there be . . . ," the creation of man assumes a different approach. The difference occurs with God saying, "Let us make man *in our image,* after our likeness, and let him have dominion over the fish of the sea, and over the fowl of the air, and over the cattle, and over all the earth, and over every creeping thing that creeps upon the earth" (1:28). This then was the purpose of creating man, who was thus assigned the responsibility over the created physical world.

The image relationship, by the very fact that it is mentioned immediately preceding the assignment, contains within it all the prerequisites necessary for man to accomplish this task—that is, reason, intellect, free will, and imagination. Image is also interpreted as "representative of God." Man thus feels the challenge to discharge that responsibility by studying nature and by extricating from it the mathematical and physical laws that operate within nature. The understanding of these laws will then permit man to control or minimize what people refer to as evils of nature, such as floods, earthquakes, and diseases. It will even allow man to transform them for positive uses, as in controlling floods, making the deserts bloom, and using windmills to generate energy. It follows that science is necessary for the dominion of nature and, therefore, is not an enemy of theology. The latest advances in medical science from the infinitesimal particles of matter to outer space attest to the ability of man to have dominion over the physical world and to discharge his responsibilities for physical existence and thereby become a partner of God. God assigned this partnership to man without giving man a choice. No need for choice was necessary because man, being the highest creation, automatically would have dominion over the physical world. God made it specific so that man would recognize that responsibility is attached to it.

It is a well-known fact that man may also destroy the balance of nature and do immeasurable harm to humanity by polluting the ground, the air, and the water for profit and selfish purposes. Thus man must be restricted in his potential abuses of nature. With free will, this could become a difficult task. The counterforce to this situation is the sense of morality and ethics that man must assume. From the Test of Adam, as discussed in previous chapters, we found that the contradictions within that narrative led Adam to conclude that God assigned to man the responsibility for the state of morality. The analysis of the choice that was presented to Adam could not lead to any other conclusion without introducing contradictions.

In life, the challenge by God that man accept responsibility for morality is ever present and attests to the presence of God in the world. Man faces choices throughout his life, either for good or for evil. God challenges him to choose good, as stated in Deuteronomy 30:19: "I have put before you life and death, blessing and the curse. Choose life if you and your offspring would live."

Chapters 1, 2, and 3 of Genesis lead to the conclusion that *man was assigned the moral responsibility of all existence in this world*. The condition of this world depends on what man chooses to do. He can accept that responsibility in the context of responsible freedom, which would result in a good life for man, or he can refuse that assignment, in which case evil and suffering would prevail. He would thus deny God and his own humanity. The problem of suffering is then in the hands of man and ceases to be a problem in theology. As Psalm 115:16 states:

The Heavens belong to the Heavens above;
The earth was given to the children of men.

This illustrates that man has the responsibility for the condition of this world. As such, man does have God in mind when making decisions involving morality. Man feels the challenge by God to resolve problems with *responsible freedom as its main underpinning*. In acting in accordance with this challenge, man actualizes God's intent.

By stating that God assigned the dominion of nature and the responsibility for morality to man, the question of God's omnipotence is not a subject for discussion. The history of man belongs to man and man alone. Those who accept the assignment must struggle with those who reject that responsibility, and the condition of the world will depend on that outcome.

In accepting God's assignment of the physical and moral dominions, we are obligated to act as a cohesive unit. Moreover, we the Jews are also unique. We are one, which excludes the other, but includes the other in his potentiality. We are a unique religion in that we consider ourselves as partners of God, the result of our autonomous choice, which no other religion claims or can claim.

The history of philosophy, the kind that is a handmaiden to theology, is a succession of conflicting views and of attempts to reconcile them. Philosophical language would describe it as a dialectical process of thesis, antithesis, and synthesis or, in religious terms, dependence, independence, and interdependence. I have discussed the traditional view, in which God is the commanding God whose commandments man has the obligation to observe. This forms the thesis or dependence of man on God. The antithesis, or independence, is to be found in humanism or existentialism, in which God is found to be superfluous in that He undercuts man's initiative and responsibility. Instead, man determines the meaning of life, since all problems are human in origin and, therefore, so are the solutions. The synthesis, or interdependence, is provided by my view that God's challenge to man is present in life to choose the responsibility for existence and become God's partner by the exercise of responsible freedom.

In line with my concept that man has the responsibility for existence in this world, we should refer to the pioneers who went to Palestine from Poland and Russia in the 1880s and 1890s and the members of the Zionist Aliyah in the early years of the twentieth century. They rejected the traditional explanation that Jewish suffering is God's punishment for Jewish sin. They refused to wait for the Messiah to "rebuild Jerusalem."

Most Jews today do not believe that Jewish suffering is God's punishment and that 6 million Jews were brutally and barbarously murdered by the Nazi criminals because of "our sins." Jews need not feel disloyal to the Jewish tradition if they reject the idea that suffering is divine punishment for sin. Explanations of this kind have consequences that are dangerous. The victim is required to assume a false consciousness regarding his fate—that is, instead of locating the source of evil in others, he views himself as the source of the evil that has befallen him.

A paradoxical version of the idea that Jews are responsible for the evil that befalls them may be seen in the critique of chosenness, i.e., in regarding themselves as chosen, the Jews have committed the sin of misanthropy or pride. This argument, not infrequently heard in Christian quarters, fails to consider that the Christians themselves believe that the covenant of chosenness has been transferred to them. One consequence of this transfer has been to exacerbate Christian anti-Semitism—a consequence that ironically calls into question the very claim Judaism advances, for a partner of God would never engage in the radical oppression of others.

My theology of responsible freedom or God-man partnership has its source in Genesis—chapters 1, 2, and 3. As such, it is unencumbered by thousands of years of sediments—be they philosophic, social, religious, cultural, political, or racial. Thus it is pristine in nature and in full accord with reason with which man was created. The Genesis account represented a revolutionary change from existing polytheistic cultures to a new concept in terms of individual justice, equality of man before the law, morality, and Weltanschauung. My theology is free from the baggage of time; it is universal in meaning and applicability and yet particularistic in that the Jews were the only ones to adopt it.

Chapter XV
The Problem of Theodicy: Freedom, Responsibility, and Evil

In the preceding chapter, a new theology was presented in which God was absolved of all evil acts in the world. This resulted from the conclusion that God assigned the responsibility for this world to man, which was derived from a new interpretation of the Adam test. While this new suggested theology serves also as a theodicy, a somewhat different theodicy is presented below in which the concept of freedom plays an important part.

The Holocaust is an unavoidable issue for contemporary Jewish theology. It is the watershed in Jewish self-understanding, forcing man to reexamine the question of God's role in history and the God-man relationship. Traditional answers to these questions thus far have failed, undermined from the outset by concepts that oppose each other with the force of contradiction, e.g., dystelogical, innocent suffering and Divine Providence. The reader interested in this subject is familiar with the innumerable attempts on the part of philosophers and theologians, discussed in an article by John Fischer.[1] Among the best known are Berkovits, Fackenheim, Maybaum, and Rubenstein. Each in his own way has tried to deal with these questions and to distill from the Holocaust some theological meaning, as shown in chapter 12.

I cannot subscribe to any currently available traditional or modern approaches to this problem. A new approach is required, one that would eliminate the contradictions and paradoxes involved and yet not deny God and His unique relationship to man. This new approach offered below is one in which God is exonerated for the evil actions of men in this world. For this purpose, a discussion of the freedom of man is necessary because the question of the theodicy of God and its inherent paradox arises essentially from the issue of freedom of man to choose evil.

Freedom is a distinctly human phenomenon. It does not belong to the inanimate world, which is completely subject to the invariant domination of physical laws. Thus a stone is not free to fall up, nor is it free not to fall down. An animal is not free to oppose its instincts. Man is the only creation of God with the unique ability to choose from any number of alternatives. Furthermore, being able to project his mind into time, he becomes aware of possible consequences of his choices, as a result of which man becomes a deliberate, conscious participant in the choice he makes. To be human, then, decisively involves man's freedom of choice and, therefore, the possibility to do good or evil. Man is free; he can choose and transcend the conditioning of his past, his environmental, economic, and other factors. It follows that *God's nonintervention is necessary for man to be man as God had created him*—that is, to make choices of his free will. We may consider that this aspect of creation was part of a divine plan to enlist man in the universal possibility for man to be a partner moving toward the goal of creation.

Human freedom and sovereignty, however, can never be absolute. Without self-imposed limits, chaos would inevitably result. Society can impose legal limits on people, but this does not guarantee moral behavior. If an individual thinks he can outwit the system and get away with overstepping the limits, he may well do so. *Only self-chosen, autonomous responsible freedom will act as a deterrent to absolute freedom; such responsibility cannot be imposed.*

Human freedom can be at one and the same time a prescription for evil deeds as well as a challenge and opportunity for good. What it will be depends on man's existential decision. Because we are born human, we have the never-ending task of having to make choices, for good or evil. Because of his ability to choose, man is responsible and is held accountable for his actions. However, it is one thing to be *responsible* for one's actions *after the act* and another thing to *approach a choice with an attitude of prior responsibility, an awareness that one has no absolute freedom in making a choice*. This latter attitude is the mark of a moral man who realizes that his choice cannot be made in a vacuum graced only by his own presence. Always there is the presence of God, who challenges man to approach the choice in the spirit of *responsible freedom*. Responsible freedom arises from accepting the attitude of prior responsibility. This is the basic responsibility of human existence. Understood in this manner, Providence and moral acts (those arising from an attitude of responsible freedom) are mutually consistent. God and man can then be seen as partners, man actualizing God's purpose for this world.

The availability of alternatives makes man's exercise of freedom meaningful. Man is free because he can transcend his conditioning and choose an opposite course. Choice, then, is the crucial issue for man because the meaning of a man's life is derived from a continual engagement in a series of choices and, therefore, of acts. A nonchoice is also a choice, and a nonact is also an act. Man does not exist in a neutral state. Through his choice, he determines the qualitative character of his existence in any given moment. Mastering evil is achieved in the very process of choosing. It is here that the confrontation in the choice between good and evil climaxes. Evil or the Divine manifest themselves in reality only when chosen and acted upon by man. Through the process of choice, man is self-determining; *if man opts for partnership with God, he adds his finite measure to the salvation of the world and in so doing confers on himself authentic existence and gives meaning and purpose to his life.*

The human drama, unfolding in the dimensions of human history and morality, is determined by man's choice. The destiny of the world hinges on what man chooses. Man's fate lies in his own hands, subject neither to the decrees of destiny nor to the guilt of his forebears. This is the consequence of the responsibility of human existence.

God, in creating man as a freely choosing human being, of necessity had to create the possibility of good and evil. Good and evil belong to the texture of nature. It follows that the possibility for good or evil actions is always present. A world without the potential for good and evil is not possible, given the conditions of our human existence—freedom and the availability of alternatives to choose from, which even includes no choice. Without the evil alternatives, people would be as puppets of God. Choice would be meaningless. We could not even choose God. Thus there would be no merit, theologically, to our existence.

The theodicy is a paradox—*man would not have a concept of a moral God if he did not know the difference between good and evil. Therefore, if God did not create the world with the possibility of evil, man's morality would not be a question to be discussed.*

The concept of partnership can be extended to the relationship between man and nature in which the advance of science as a means of alleviating the human condition could be understood in light of the obligation to "master nature" (1:28). The fact that modern technology has often been used in the service of evil ends is not a statement about the nature of science or technology, but a statement, if not an indictment, of the human will behind it. The question of man as a moral agent (or partner of God) thus remains primary. It is to that question, then, that we must turn.

It is in the social sphere in which suffering is so prevalent that the problem of theodicy—the apparent conflict between the existence of evil and the presence of an omnipotent and just God—is most difficult to understand. This is because the problem is full of contradictions and paradoxes, where God and man seem to be adversaries and where faith confronts experience. This question has permeated Jewish literature. To cite only one example, Abraham, the Patriarch of the Jewish faith, questions God on this very issue:

> Will You sweep away the innocent along with the guilty? Far be it from You to do such a thing, to bring death upon the innocent as well as the guilty, so that innocent and guilty fare alike. Far be it from You! Shall not the Judge of all the earth deal justly?
> —Genesis 18:23–25

The question of theodicy is thus introduced with God's own acquiescence, as demonstrated by His patience with Abraham's persistent questioning. The basic issue has been joined—*the unquestioning faith in God and man's sense of justice and morality.* Job, in demanding an explanation from God, since he considered himself blameless, fell silent before God's power and omnipotence. His questions remained unanswered, but his faith remained intact. This represents the ultimate traditional view of faith: "Even though He slay me, yet will I believe in Him" (Job). Thus Job did not act as a partner of God.

Job's view is not the view of Abraham in the binding of Isaac's story. Abraham submitted the demand to the question of morality and was able to resolve the contradictions in the story without denying God and His justice.[2]

Historically, every traditional solution to the seeming paradox had as its primary goal the justification of God. The status of the deity had to be protected. Every traditional attempt to answer the question, "Why does God permit evil acts and why do righteous people suffer?" falls apart on the rocks of inherent contradictions and the conflict of free choice, faith, reason, and God working in history. Even the first part of the question, "Why does God permit evil deeds?," is contradictory to the notion of

God acting in history. If God acts in history, the presence of evil acts is not only a part of His plan, but may be evidence that He condones it, and even that He causes it. In this sense, God would be responsible for the Holocaust! The second part of the question assumes a necessary connection, a cause-and-effect relationship, between righteousness and reward, and between evil deeds and punishment. This may not indeed be the case, as the condition of man in this world seems to indicate. Faith in God, as God of justice, demands it, nevertheless. Job, in his insistence on his righteousness and in demanding an explanation, did not see any cause and effect situation but fell silent in the face of the omnipotence of God.

Is there a solution? I suggest there is. I will present a theological model for the resolution of this seemingly unsolvable problem in which God's covenantal relationship to man is maintained, evil acts are not God's responsibility, and reason is not forfeited to faith. In this, I shall follow the common basic rule of all thinking, that inconsistencies and contradictions must be avoided, and which I claim has not been the case to date.

If God gave man the freedom to choose, can God then be held responsible for evil acts of man? In part A, chapter III, I reinterpreted the Test of Adam as a creation of the potential moral and spiritual man. I showed that the action by Adam was not a sin, as has been interpreted for some two thousand years, and which forms the doctrine of Original Sin in Christianity. In view of the negative command with its inherent contradictions (one of those contradictions being that man can be a moral being without the knowledge of good and evil), it was concluded that God wanted man to choose the knowledge of good and evil and, furthermore, to do so through his own free and autonomous decision and thus become a moral and spiritual being. The purpose of the test of Adam was to assign the moral and spiritual domain to man.[3] The created man is thus ordained into the struggle for salvation as one who is himself called upon to choose between good and evil alternatives.

The power of decision was entrusted to man. With his choice, Adam embarked upon an earthly path. The test of Adam revealed the goal, the destiny, that God intended for mankind. Man was to become the partner of God in the world (3:5, 3:22), giving rise to a relationship of a higher order than that of power involved in a Creator and creature relationship. Adam was to become like God, but not God. Being like God, knowing good and evil, man can leave Paradise and take charge of the world as a partner of God. Adam's choice can be said to be a primal choice. The words *God* and *choice* are primary words. Everything flows from them. They form the connection between the divine and man, and between Heaven and the human world. For man to become a partner of God, he must choose for himself this task and affirm it. In so doing, he confers on himself authentic existence. *The Adam story reveals God as the Challenger to all people to accept the knowledge of good and evil and thus assume the responsibility for the moral condition of this world. The eternal presence of God attests to the eternal presence of the challenge.*

God's faith in man's capability to act as a partner of God is shown in Genesis 2:19, prior to the test of Adam:

> And the Lord God formed out of the earth all the wild beasts and all the birds of the sky, and brought them to the man to see what he would call them . . .

God forms the animals, but He enlists man in the creative activity of naming them, a process of transcendence that, in the ancient world, meant conferring meaning and significance, as well as lordship. Man was asked to complete God's process of creation, which certainly represents a partnership idea.

The physical world, including man, was created by God without requiring human participation—consequently, man was created last. In contrast, the world of meaning in the process of naming was the task assigned to man, and thus Adam II (the creation in chapter 2 of Genesis) was created first, his contribution fully required. God and man thus stand together in an intimate partnership. God manifests Himself in the challenge of responsibility, while man answers in the affirmative, "Here I am." By this answer we give ourselves an identity.

God, while investing in man the freedom to choose, nevertheless gives him direction of choice to be made:

Surely if you do right,
There is uplift.
But if you do not do right
Sin is the demon at the door,
Whose urge is toward you
Yet you can be its master.
—Genesis 4:7

It is thus emphasized that it is man's responsibility as an expression of his partnership role to be the master of his choice and that the right choice results in uplift. Another illustration of Torah's intention for man's choice is expressed in the following lines:

I have put before you life and death, blessing and curse. Choose life if you and your offspring would live.
—Deuteronomy 30:19

Man, as a partner of God, must turn his attention to this world. In accepting God's challenge and assignment of this world, and in assuming the partnership, man expresses his active commitment to this world. Every human arena becomes man's responsibility, and every act becomes a spiritual expression of his partnership role.

The above is not advocating a humanistic approach to life. Simply stated, the humanistic approach rests on the premise that all of man's problems are human in origin and in solution. God is banned from this world because God undercuts man's initiative and responsibility; furthermore, man is at the mercy of forces held to be outside his control! In the humanistic approach, if any God is admitted to exist, He is functionless as far as man's destiny is concerned.

The partner of God, on the other hand, approaches the solution from the viewpoint of God-given inalienable rights, the assignment of this world to man and his acceptance of responsibility for it. Man is not then the measure of his own values, because in the acceptance of responsibility God's challenge is required in every deliberation and solution of problems.

The Adam story is the first story of the first man, and the story is that of choice. Adam was born to choose between two alternatives, a sort of two-dimensional freedom. In choosing the knowledge of good and evil, Adam became truly free—free in depth as well. This dimension of freedom imposes limits on itself for the sake of true (responsible) freedom and opposes absolute freedom.

This difference between absolute freedom and responsible freedom gives the lie to radical theology, which sees God and man as competitors, even enemies. It is either man or God. Man has come of age and in freedom accepts responsibility for his life and the world (or he is free to enslave others). Man becomes the supreme being. He deifies himself in that he sets his own standards, which are in reality no standards, because the community component is absent. His responsibility is only to himself. Without responsible freedom, i.e., partnership with God, everything is possible. Man certainly proved this in Auschwitz. According to the radical theologians, man is free and responsible for the consequences of his actions. However, he does not approach problems from a sense of prior responsibility and limited freedom. This is the essential difference.

My thesis claims that God indeed cannot work fully in history. God can work in history only by virtue of the partnership relationship that man establishes in accepting the challenge of God, but He cannot work through the evil man precisely because he, the evil man, rejects God's challenge and assignment of the moral sphere to man. The disassociation of God from being the director of history and from man's inhumanity to man exculpates God of His involvement in the Holocaust. As Edmund Burke said two centuries ago: "The only thing necessary for the triumph of evil is for good men to do nothing." In the Holocaust period, we see this in the action, or rather nonaction, of the leaders of the world, be they the pope, Roosevelt, Churchill, church leaders, philosophers, and humanists in Germany itself, and the indifference of the population of the world, all of whom abdicated their responsibility and thus allowed the Holocaust to happen. At the very beginning, Hitler could have been stopped and his radical evil prevented by the actions of men and nations. Their disinterest, as Hitler had learned from the experience of the Armenians at the hands of the Turks, made the Holocaust possible. The disinterest of the people and its consequence is well stated by Pastor Niemoller:

> In Germany, the Nazis first came for the Communists, and I didn't speak up because I was not a Communist. Then they came for the Jews and I did not speak up because I was not a Jew. Then they came for the Trade Unionists and I did not speak up because I was not a Trade Unionist. Then they came for me . . . by that time, there was no one to speak up for anyone.

God will not work in history to prevent evil acts, just as He will not prevent the emergence of false gods and prophets. This is a necessary consequence of God's creating man with a free will.

The traditional explanation for the suffering of the Jewish people has been: "For our sins we have been punished." This doctrine makes the victim responsible for his suffering.

It is obscene to claim that the Holocaust was God's punishment for our sins. This is a result of the belief that God acts directly in history. The unfolding of history is man's responsibility assigned to him by God, and therefore God cannot be blamed for the Holocaust. The biblical God who requires human help in making goodness prevail is a better response to the problem of evil and the Holocaust than is the God of theologians requiring omnipotence, justice, and goodness. The biblical God charges man to master and subdue nature, assigns the moral sphere to man, and charges man to accept partnership with God voluntarily and autonomously. Thus man would act with an attitude of responsibility. He would fully devote himself to this task only if it is chosen autonomously, for this choice would represent his inner and complete self. Man must want to choose this duty for him to discharge it and to be effective. If man, in his freedom, rejects this attitude, he rejects God and he enters the world of evil. God's purpose in history is thus nullified.

The Holocaust occurred because of or in spite of God (in either case theologically unacceptable), and only we, the Jewish people, the only group perceiving itself in the unique relationship with God, that of partnership, must redeem ourselves and the world. This was the purpose in the Adam II story where man was assigned the responsibility for the morality of the world.

Theological efforts that attempt to filter the events of history through the prism of Divine Providence substitute a greater unknown for the lesser one—a method that would not be acceptable in any other field of disciplined inquiry. The alternative, however, is not to sever the Divine and human orders completely. No theology with so radical a separation as its premise could legitimatize itself as Jewish. What is necessary is to understand

Divine Providence in history through the human agency that creates history, to recognize that man stands in a partnership with God, the very terms of which make man responsible for his fate. The essential role of Providence is metaphysically to constitute man with the freedom to choose this responsibility as a partner of God. The rest belongs to man, given this premise. The truth of Judaism's mode of self-interpretation lies in affirming the Jewish people's unique relationship with God, that of partnership or "choosing" God's challenge of the responsibility of existence.

Notes

1. "God after the Holocaust: An Attempted Reconciliation," *Judaism*, 32, no. 3 (Summer 1983 issue, issue 121): 309.
2. See Part A, chapter 5: "The Akedah: A Test of Abraham as a Partner of God."
3. See Part A, chapters 2 and 3, of this book for greater details and argumentation.

Afterword

For almost thirty years Sidney Breitbart has been an ardent student of Judaism. Far from being satisfied with occasional sermons and homiletic interpretations of Judaism, Sidney applied himself to Jewish scholarship. In addition, he sponsors Jewish scholarship and scholars. Devotion to scholarly study by a successful businessman is practically unknown today, certainly in the way Sidney carries out his mission. He remains as systematic in his Judaic studies as he was in his engineering profession, with a graduate degree from Columbia University, and in his other business pursuits.

Since the mid-1960s, Sidney has travelled some thirty miles each week from his home in Aberdeen to classes at Baltimore Hebrew University. When he retired from business, he established a second home in Baltimore. During these years, Sidney attended classes in the graduate, undergraduate, and Continuing Education schools, and while he enjoyed every field of Jewish study, his special love was philosophy.

His classes in philosophy involved Jewish thought, but within the context of European thought. His reading and thinking ranged far, but they always returned to an issue that plagued and bedeviled him—God's relationship to humans and, more specifically, the issue of human responsibility, which he touched on in his earliest articles. He was never satisfied and repeatedly returned to the problem of the original God-man relationship described in the first chapters of the Book of Genesis. As time passsed, Sidney's struggle with the problem of divine and human justice intensified: why do the innocent, let alone the righteous, suffer? (Sidney is sagacious enough not to waste time in asking why the wicked prosper: they do.)

Sidney sees life through the prism of the Jewish intellectual heritage. His questions are Jewish religious questions, but his responses are not traditional answers; they are his own. He believes that the answers are hidden in the first few chapters of Genesis and, therefore, has devoted himself to exegesis of those chapters. He sees in them the meaning of the relationship between God and man, and between man and man.

In reading Sidney's essays, it also becomes clear that God's role was to turn over responsibility of the world, both physical and moral, to man. As a result, the answer to the question of why do the righteous suffer has to be found in an assessment of the conduct of people and human society, not as a claim against God. The Holocaust resulted in the murder of 6 million Jews and countless others because of the Third Reich, not because of God's absence. God did not hide His face; man did.

Sidney's accusation extends beyond the murders themselves. He holds the teachings that produced German Christian Jew hatred responsible for a society that countenanced and participated in the killing. Here Sidney turns to one of his strongest points in which he entwines his general theory of human responsibility, going back to Adam, with his critique of society. He finds in Christian teaching a significant absence of understanding human responsibility. While medieval and late ancient Christian teachings are well known for their anti-Judaism, it is only recently that the role of Paul has been examined. Sidney points directly to Pauline teaching, but not to an anti-Jewish sentiment. He takes issue with the antinomianism of Paul, which he views as lacking the ethical and legal responsibility that controls society.

This book is a collection of essays that lead to a general concept, but not a conclusion, of Sidney's writings and thoughts.

He was prodded by his friends to compile his essays as an important subtotal of his work. It would be a mistake to believe that he will spend much time reading this book in which he should take great pride. Knowing Sidney, he will continue working on other exegesical problems.

Having mentioned Sidney as a sponsor of scholarship and scholars, but aware of his modesty, it is important to point out that he generously endowed the finest scholarship available. He never considered a gift to the university to be his last one. His sponsorship is a direct investment in the perpetuation of Jewish thought as only a careful businessman can make. It should be said, above all, that Sidney's philanthropy includes an abundance of time. As a trustee and officer of the board of Baltimore Hebrew University, he was present during its finest decades—wonderful years which he helped bring into being.

—Dr. Leivy Smolar
President
Baltimore Hebrew University
1971–1992

Index

Abraham
  monotheism, 38
  qualifications for being chosen, 80
  encounters with God, 37, 38
  Sodom and Gomorrah, 40
  the Akedah and its resolution, 37–48
  comparison with Job, 118
Abraham Ibn Daud
  God cannot be the cause of both good and evil, 111
Adam I
  image relationships, 3, 4
  the charge by God, 4
  indication of mortality, 8
Adam II
  the creation of Adam II, 5
  the difference in the order of creation of Adam I and Adam II, 6
  the Tree of Knowledge of Good and Evil, 5, 6, 112
  the rivers in the Garden, 7
  the creation of Eve, 8
  the prohibition about the Tree, 6
  naming of the animals, 5, 8
Akedah
  the problem in isolation, 37
  Abraham as the passive, silent beneficiary of God's promises, 38
  spiritual development of Abraham, 38, 39, 40
  covenant of circumcision, 39
  the "immoral" demand, 40, 41
  the journey of anguish, 41–44
  dilemma facing Abraham, 44
  the resolution of the test, 44, 45
  Sarah and Isaac, 46
Albright, William F.
  evil inherited from animals, 13
  rejection of this view, 13, 14
Amos, 64, 85
anti-Semitism
  religious, 92
  Christian role, 96, 97
  Luther's role, 97
Augustine
  doctrine of original sin, 11, 13
  evil and perfidy of the Jews, 96
  privation theory, 102

Berkowits, Eliezer
  God controlling His infinite power in the Holocaust, 114
  arguments against it, 114
Buber, Martin
  God hiding His face in the Holocaust, 104
Burke, Edmund, 139

Cain
  the first sin in history, 23
choice
  freedom of choice, 30
  in the Adam II narrative, 31
  in Teshuvah, 67
  in repentance, 67
  in moral problems, 20
  wrong choices as a logical necessity, 106, 107
chosen people
  traditional views, 76
  M. M. Kaplan's view, 76
  new view—Jew chooses God, 78, 82
  prerequisites necessary for chosenness, 78
  Rubenstein's stance, 113
Christianity
  disobedience of Adam II, 11

original sin, 11
   Adam's action not a sin—a new view, 20, 21, 22
   Christian teachings and the culture of Fallen Man—a foundation for Shoah, 94, 97
Chrysostom
   anti-Semitic views, 96
Clement of Alexandria
   moral freedom and responsibility, 12
   carnal knowledge, 12
communal responsibility
   revelatory sense of community, 93, 94
   Jewish view, 21, 32
covenant
   development of covenant, 56, 57, 58
   a new interpretation, 59, 60, 61, 85, 86
   God-man partnership, 60, 61
   Christian covenant and its untenability, 86
   the new concept of covenant as a universal view, 88
Crescas, Hasdai
   reward and punishment, 110
   counterarguments, 110

deicide
   Christian claim, 70
   cause for anti-Semitism, 70

evil
   God and evil—part of texture of nature, 7, 103
   natural evil, 101
   moral-free will, 101
   self-inflicted—man's choice, 12

Fackenheim, Emil
   root experience, 114
   God entering into finiteness, 51, 52, 60
   withdrawal of God, 114
final solution for the Jews
   implication of, 69, 70
   Holocaust, 69, 70, 84
finitude of man
   preordained, 32
forgiveness
   Wiesenthal's question, 68, 73
   requirement for forgiveness, 67
   the role of the victims, 71, 73
   nature of crime, 68, 74
   lack of forgiveness for "Jewish part in deicide," 74
   Memory as a shield against reoccurrence—"Never Again," 71
freedom
   two-dimensional, 30
   responsible freedom, 30

Garden of Eden, 5
Genesis 1
   creation of nature, 3
   creation of man in the image of God, 3
   assignment of physical world to man, 3
Genesis 2
   creation of Adam II, 6
   the Tree of Knowledge of Good and Evil, 6, 7, 11
   naming the animals, 5, 8
   creation of Eve, 8
   the threat of death in God's order, 6
   factors influencing Adam's choice, 20, 21
   assignment of the moral sphere to man, 30, 126, 127
   expulsion from the Garden, 104
God
   as creator, 3, 5
   as challenger to man, 3, 32, 33, 53, 106
   assignment of the world to man, 3, 32

God-man partnership, 4, 16, 32, 33, 54, 129
God during the Holocaust
   Buber's view, 104, 105
   Berkowits's view, 114
Grant, Michael
   Paul's view of man, 93
   Paul's view of law, 92
   Paul's view of salvation, 93
   Paul's view of faith, 92
Gregory of Nissa
   the nature of the soul, 12

Halevi, Judah
   election of Israel by merit, 26, 85
Hillers, Delbert R.
   the distinctiveness of the covenant, 57
Holocaust
   deicide charge, 95
   Jewish chosenness replaced by Christians, 95
   anti-Semitism, 96
   indifference in Europe, 73
   silence of the church, 95
   the differences between the covenants as a source, 94
   as a challenge to Christianity, 94, 95
   Buber's view, 104, 105
   and memory, 71
human existence
   binary order of existence, 103
   tensional—physical and moral, 125
humanism, 35
Hume, David
   God and evil as incompatible, 115, 116

Isaiah, 87

Job
   wager between God and Adversary, 118, 119
   description of Job, 119
   guilt by acts of omission, 119
   community responsibility, 118
   contrast with Abraham, 118
   as a subjective problem, 123
   inconsistence in Job's questions, 120
   suffering and sin, 121
   God's response compared to His response to Abraham, 121
   man as the source of evil, 122
Justin (martyr)
   allegience to God of humanity (creator), 11

Kant, Immanuel
   autonomy of man, 32

Leibnitz, Gottfried Wilhelm
   best of all possible worlds, 116
Littel, Franklin H.
   "Was Jesus a false Messiah?", 95
Luther, Martin
   Jewish refusal to follow Luther, 72
   charges against Jews—the language of Naziism, 72
   reference to Luther as justification for Nazi actions, 70

Maimonides, Moses
   intellect vs. practical knowledge, 10, 26
   matter as a concommittant of privation—the cause of evil, 102, 103, 110
   justice of God, 103
   fall of Adam, 26
   Genesis and destruction, 104
man
   in the image of God, 3, 4
   reason, 3
   free choice, 3
   perfection, 10
   dominion of physical world, 4

autonomous responsibility of the moral sphere, 32
man as a sinner—Christian view, 87
interdependence of God and man, 128
Maritain, Jacques
"In the name of your God, I forgive you," 74
Matthew, 88, 89
Maybaum, Ignatz
remnant as opposed to Final Solution, 115
Messiah, 15, 95
morality
knowledge of difference between good and evil, 14
God's purpose in the test of Adam II, 20
choice by man, 11, 18
man's responsibility for morality, 74
Moses
as agent to bring a nation into being, 79, 81
myth
meaning in our context, 16

Nachmanides, Moses, 119, 120
nature
animal, 13, 29
human and choice, 10, 12, 29, 30
in Christianity, 13, 93
good and evil—a part of the texture of nature, 112

original sin
Jewish view—sin is not inherited, 10
Christian doctrine, 11
corruption of all nature, 13
repudiates the good of God's creation, 12
repudiates the freedom of human will, 12

Ozick, Cynthia
on forgiveness, 69

Parkes, James
interpretation of the Law, 89
partnership of God and man, 4, 16, 32, 33, 54, 129
Paul
on Law, 89
new covenant of faith, 90
"Sin is lifeless without law," 91
the failure of Paul's logic—the reestablishment of Israel, 90, 91
prayer
basis of prayer, 63
origin, 63, 64
essence, 66
types and range of prayer, 63, 64
function in new theology, 65, 66
prophets, 55
punishment of Adam
expulsion from Garden of Eden, 104
work in hostile environment, 24
pain in childbirth, 23
argument against punishment, 7, 23–25

Radical Theology
responsible freedom vs. absolute freedom, 138
Ramsey, Paul
the importance of covenant, 85
redemption
Jewish view, 87, 93
Christian view, 88
man's functions, 87
creed vs. deed, 92
repentance
general requirement for, 67
by an SS man on his deathbed, 68, 73
lack of repentance on the part of the church, 70

responsibility
  after an action and prior to action, 132
  in man's choices, 132
  Jewish view, 87
Revelation
  the scope and possibility, 51
  communication between the finite and infinite, 52
  creation as revelation, 52
  image relationship as revelation, 53
  challenge of knowledge of good and evil—as revelation, 53
reward and punishment—retribute theology
  Jewish view, 101, 102
  arguments against, 109, 110
Rinser, Louise
  "... for they know not what they do," 73
  "God, God, why have you forsaken me?", 74
Rubenstein, Richard
  God as director of history, 113
  blaming God for evil, 113

Saadya Gaon
  his view of evil, 111
salvation
  Jewish view, 87
  Christian view, 88
Sartre, Jean Paul
  the existential "I", 31, 32
Schweitzer, Albert
  view of Paul's ethics, 92
secular view
  opposed to religion, 34
  creation and the Adam II test—new view, 34, 35
sin
  sin in the test of Adam II, 8, 10, 11, 14
  first sin—the Abel and Cain narrative, 23

Sodom and Gomorrah
  Abraham's persistent questioning, 40
suffering
  philosophic problem, 104
  natural kinds, 108
  moral kinds, 108
  man's responsibility, 127
  false consciousness regarding the Jewish people's fate, 129

teshuvah
  repentance, 67
  choice to change from evil to good, 67
test of Adam
  God's purpose, 8, 18, 19
  contradictions in the narrative, 18
  Adam's analysis, 17–21
  factors in the narrative predicting the outcome, 7, 8
  first choice as the philosophical first thing, 30
  first choice in history—a positive dimension, 28
  responsibility for the moral realm, 30
  the depth dimension of freedom—responsible freedom, 30
  mortality and partnership with God, 32
theodicy
  as a paradox, 133, 134
  choice, 131
  responsible freedom as a deterrent to absolute freedom, 131
  God's assignment of morality to man, 136
  partner of God, 133, 136
  the world belongs to man, 133
theological resolution of the problem of evil
  God's challenge to man, 3, 21

    responsible freedom, 127
    God-man partnership, 28, 126
    binary character of existence, 103
    man's choice, 126, 127
    acceptance of responsibility by man, 127, 128, 135
    suffering, 127
Tolstoy, Leo, 36
Torah (law)
    role in Judaism, 54, 55
    role in Christianity, 90
Tree of Knowledge of Good and Evil
    basis of morality, 20
    existence of good and evil as part of texture of nature, 7, 103

Tree of Life
    the Torah, 25
tsimtsum
    contraction of God, 105

Van Buren, Paul
    factors responsible for Christian theological reappraisal, 95

will of God
    view in God-man partnership, 32, 78, 107
    responsible freedom, 30, 107